THE
UNOFFICIAL
SIMS
COOKBOOK

From Baked Alaska to Silly Gummy Bear Pancakes,
85+ Recipes to Satisfy the HUNGER NEED

TAYLOR O'HALLORAN

ADAMS MEDIA

NEW YORK   LONDON   TORONTO   SYDNEY   NEW DELHI

Adams Media
An Imprint of Simon & Schuster, Inc.
100 Technology Center Drive
Stoughton, Massachusetts 02072

First Adams Media hardcover edition
October 2022

ADAMS MEDIA and colophon are trademarks of Simon & Schuster.

For information about special discounts for bulk purchases, please contact Simon & Schuster Special Sales at 1-866-506-1949 or business@simonandschuster.com.

The Simon & Schuster Speakers Bureau can bring authors to your live event. For more information or to book an event contact the Simon & Schuster Speakers Bureau at 1-866-248-3049 or visit our website at www.simonspeakers.com.

Interior design by Julia Jacintho
Interior images © 123RF/mything, sudowoodo
Photographs by Harper Point Photography
Photography Chefs: Christine Tarango, Abraham Lemus, Trevor Laymance

Manufactured in the
United States of America

3 2022

Library of Congress Cataloging-in-Publication Data
Names: O'Halloran, Taylor, author.
Title: The unofficial Sims cookbook / Taylor O'Halloran.
Description: First Adams Media hardcover edition. | Stoughton, Massachusetts: Adams Media, 2022 | Series: Unofficial cookbook | Includes index.
Identifiers: LCCN 2022014634 | ISBN 9781507219454 (hc) | ISBN 9781507219461 (ebook)
Subjects: LCSH: Cooking. | Sims (Video game) | LCGFT: Cookbooks.
Classification: LCC TX714 .O343 2022 | DDC 641.5--dc23/eng/20220607
LC record available at https://lccn.loc.gov/2022014634

ISBN 978-1-5072-1945-4
ISBN 978-1-5072-1946-1 (ebook)

DEDICATION

This book is dedicated to my mother, Sonia, for igniting my love for The Sims; to my sister, Brooke, for keeping it going; and to my fiancé, Chris, for always believing in me. Oh, and to my brother, Justin, for allowing me to always send him to military school in *The Sims 1*.

CONTENTS

CHAPTER FOUR
SIDES...87

CHAPTER FIVE
DESSERTS...108

CHAPTER SIX
BEVERAGES...155

INTRODUCTION

Sul sul! Have you ever been playing The Sims and thought, "Wow, that Chef's Salad looks scrumptious," or "I really need to try Ratatouille someday"? Then *The Unofficial Sims Cookbook* was made for you.

Food has been a huge part of The Sims for decades, affecting your Sims' lives in so many ways, from Ambrosia saving your Sims from death, to a quick Caesar Salad coming to the rescue when your Sims forget to pay their bills and the Landgraabs turn off their power. And whether it be a luscious serving of Lobster Thermidor cooked to impress the private school Headmaster in *The Sims 2*, or some Minty Mocha Cupcakes made on the cupcake machine in *The Sims 4*, Simmers want to create these delicious recipes for themselves.

In *The Unofficial Sims Cookbook*, Sims content creator Taylor O'Halloran and author and recipe developer Kelly Jaggers take eighty-eight of your favorite recipes from the game and transform them into something you can make from the comfort of your own kitchen. The best part? You don't even need to level up your cooking skill to get started. The recipes you'll see range from quick and simple dishes like Grilled Cheese (Chapter 2) to more involved meals that Bob Pancakes would make if he could ever become the master chef he's always dreamed of being. (Too bad Eliza always seems to get in the way of his dreams.)

In this cookbook, you'll find recipes for any occasion in your (or your Sim's) life, including:

- A delicious **Banana Pancakes** (Chapter 1) recipe for your first day of private school.

- A perfect lunch recipe for **Garlic Noodles** (Chapter 2) to feed your date before attending the Romance Festival.

- A beautiful **Roast Chicken** (Chapter 3) dinner recipe that is sure to impress the Goths at your next dinner party.

- A **Cheese Eyeballs** (Chapter 4) side dish recipe that will scare Vlad when he appears at your doorstep tonight.

- Classic **Black and White Cookies** (Chapter 5) to serve at your Sim's wedding to Johnny Zest.

- A classy **Simsmapolitan** (Chapter 6) beverage recipe for your next night on the town.

You'll also discover fun facts about The Sims franchise that you can share with your loved ones as you feed them your comforting Mac and Cheese (Chapter 2).

These recipes will impress Simmers and non-Simmers alike and are meant to be enjoyed and then created again in-game because, as all Simmers know, you can't keep everything in the real world. These virtual characters are an extension of yourself, and now you can experience many of the dishes your Sims love to eat each and every day you play. You'll be inspired to cook these dishes and eat them while you sit at your computer making your Sims have another baby to try to save their marriage. Happy cooking (and playing)!

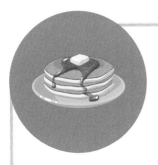

BREAKFAST

Breakfast is arguably the most important meal of the day. What you have for breakfast can set the tone for the rest of the day. Are you going to be feeling **fine**? **Happy**? **Energized**? Your first meal can have a serious impact on your mood for the day, so having options is very important. Quick meals for breakfast every day (like cereal or toast) will leave both you and your Sims feeling unsatisfied and uncomfortable. Breakfast is also a great place to start if you're just getting into cooking IRL and don't yet have a high level of **cooking** skill. Starting with breakfast can help you gain confidence in the kitchen without having to work with complicated ingredients.

In this chapter, you'll find all sorts of delicious breakfast options for your busy mornings, including nutritious meals like High-Energy Protein Plates and unique treats for your taste buds like Silly Gummy Bear Pancakes. Whatever you choose, you are going to have an awesome morning, so psych yourself up in the mirror, head to your kitchen, and get cooking.

SILLY GUMMY BEAR PANCAKES
The Sims 4

If you ever find yourself with an extra-strong, playful moodlet early in the morning, the only cure may be a serving of Silly Gummy Bear Pancakes. These pancakes will have you and your family smiling all day; just make sure you don't eat too many, or you might get hysterical.

Serves:	Prep Time:	Cook Time:
4	10 minutes	20 minutes

2 cups baking mix, such as Bisquick Pancake and Baking Mix

½ teaspoon baking soda

1 cup buttermilk

2 large eggs

1 tablespoon unsalted butter, melted and cooled

1 teaspoon pure vanilla extract

2 tablespoons vegetable oil

1 cup small gummy bears, divided

4 tablespoons unsalted butter, at room temperature

1 cup pancake syrup

1 Preheat oven to 170°F and place a metal cooling rack on a baking sheet in oven to warm up.

2 In a medium bowl, whisk together baking mix and baking soda.

3 In a separate medium bowl, whisk together buttermilk, eggs, melted butter, and vanilla. Pour wet ingredients into dry ingredients and stir until well mixed and no lumps remain. Set aside.

4 Heat a medium nonstick skillet over medium heat. Once hot, dip a paper towel into oil and lightly coat bottom of pan. Use a lightly greased ⅓-cup measuring cup to pour 2–3 pancakes into skillet. Cook 30 seconds, then gently press four or five gummy bears into top of each pancake. Cook 1 minute or until pancake edges appear dry, bubbles begin to form on top, and bottom of pancake is golden brown.

5 Flip pancakes and cook another 60–70 seconds until other side is golden brown and pancake springs back when gently pressed in center. Transfer cooked pancakes to prepared baking sheet and keep warm in oven while you repeat with remaining batter and gummy bears.

Continued on next page

6   To serve, stack two pancakes on each plate.
    Top each stack with 1 tablespoon butter and ¼ cup
    syrup. Garnish with remaining gummy bears.
    Serve immediately.

Did You Know?

In *The Sims 4*, if a Sim gets too many playful moodlets,
they have a chance of feeling hysterical—and if you allow
your Sims to feel hysterical for too long, they may die
from their extreme emotions. You can stop this by having
your Sims either calm themselves down in the mirror or
do a non-playful task!

FRENCH TOAST

The Sims 3 and *The Sims 4*

French Toast is a staple breakfast if you have a sweet tooth, and this recipe will not disappoint. Even though the name says "French," you don't need to take a trip to Champs Les Sims to create this delicious meal; you can make it in the comfort of your home.

Serves:	Prep Time:	Cook Time:
4	5 minutes	25 minutes

½ cup whole milk

2 large eggs

1 teaspoon ground cinnamon

1 teaspoon pure vanilla extract

2 tablespoons vegetable oil

8 slices thick-cut bread, such as Texas toast or brioche

¼ cup confectioners' sugar

1 cup mixed fresh berries, such as blueberries and sliced strawberries

1 Preheat oven to 170°F and place a metal cooling rack on a baking sheet in oven to warm.

2 In a medium bowl, whisk together milk, eggs, cinnamon, and vanilla. Set aside.

3 Heat a medium nonstick skillet over medium heat. Once hot, dip a paper towel into oil and lightly coat bottom of pan.

4 Dip 2 slices bread into egg mixture, making sure both sides are evenly coated. Place in prepared skillet and cook 2–3 minutes until golden brown.

5 Flip bread and cook another 2–3 minutes until golden brown on other side. Transfer to prepared baking sheet and keep warm in oven while you repeat cooking with remaining 6 slices bread.

6 To serve, slice French toast into triangles and arrange on a serving platter. Dust with sugar and garnish with berries. Serve warm.

FRIED PEANUT BUTTER AND BANANA SANDWICH

The Sims 3

If you're a fan of peanut butter and banana sandwiches, you'll die for a fried PB&B. This meal is the perfect breakfast on a gloomy fall morning when you just don't want to get out of bed and would rather spend your day watching *Lost Dog's Journey Home* than going to work. Frying this sandwich melts the peanut butter in such a way that you will be craving this for weeks.

Serves:	Prep Time:	Cook Time:
1	5 minutes	4 minutes

3 tablespoons creamy peanut butter

2 slices white sandwich bread

½ medium banana, peeled and sliced

1 tablespoon unsalted butter

1 Heat a medium nonstick pan over medium heat.

2 Spread peanut butter evenly on each bread slice. Lay banana slices on one slice and top with second slice, peanut butter–side down.

3 Add butter to pan. Once melted and foaming, add sandwich. Cook 2 minutes per side or until each side is crisp and golden brown.

4 Transfer sandwich to a large plate and cool 2 minutes before enjoying.

BREAKFAST SCRAMBLE

The Sims 4: Outdoor Retreat

A perfect meal for cooking newbies, even Bob and Betty Newbie could master this simple dish. You can completely customize your scramble with whatever ingredients you enjoy or whichever ones you found in the local gardener's backyard. Even better? This dish is great when cooked in Granite Falls over a nice campfire!

Serves:	Prep Time:	Cook Time:
2	10 minutes	23 minutes

4 large eggs

¼ teaspoon salt

¼ teaspoon ground black pepper

2–3 dashes (⅛ teaspoon each) hot sauce, optional

4 ounces bulk pork or turkey breakfast sausage

1 cup Ore-Ida frozen potatoes with onions and peppers

1 cup sliced button mushrooms

1. Preheat oven to 350°F.

2. In a large bowl, combine eggs, salt, and pepper. Add hot sauce, if desired, and stir well. Set aside.

3. In a medium nonstick skillet over medium heat, add sausage. Cook, crumbling into ½"-sized pieces, until browned and cooked through, about 8 minutes. Transfer sausage crumbles to a paper towel–lined plate and set aside. Leave drippings in skillet.

4. Add potatoes to skillet and cook 4 minutes. Add mushrooms and cook, stirring frequently, until tender and potatoes are golden, about 6–8 minutes.

5. Add sausage back to skillet, then add egg mixture and cook, stirring often, until eggs are set, about 3 minutes. Transfer to two plates and serve hot.

A Simple Swap

You can find Ore-Ida's Potatoes O'Brien (potatoes with onion and peppers) in the frozen foods section of your grocery story. If this is not available, you can swap for ¾ cup frozen hash browns with 2 tablespoons chopped onion and 2 tablespoons chopped green bell pepper.

SPINACH FRITTATA
The Sims 4

Sometimes a member of the household is living a junk food fiend lifestyle and it's hard to get them to eat their greens. Well, a Spinach Frittata is a great place to hide some delicious veggies in that Sims breakfast. All of the other ingredients will make this meal so delicious they won't even notice the spinach!

Serves:	Prep Time:	Cook Time:
6	5 minutes	32 minutes

8 large eggs

⅓ cup half-and-half

½ teaspoon salt

½ teaspoon ground black pepper

⅛ teaspoon ground nutmeg

1½ cups shredded sharp Cheddar cheese, divided

1 tablespoon unsalted butter

½ medium yellow onion, finely diced (about ½ cup)

4 ounces (about 4 packed cups) fresh baby spinach

1   Preheat oven to 350°F.

2   In a large bowl, add eggs, half-and-half, salt, pepper, and nutmeg. Whisk until well combined. Stir in 1 cup cheese and set aside.

3   In a 10" oven-safe skillet over medium heat, add butter. Once melted and foaming, add onion and cook until just tender, about 2 minutes. Add spinach and cook, stirring often, until wilted, about 2 minutes.

4   Arrange vegetables evenly over bottom of skillet. Pour egg and cheese mixture over top, then gently tilt pan to ensure eggs coat pan evenly. Cook 2 minutes without stirring.

5   Transfer skillet to oven and bake 18–22 minutes until eggs are set in center.

6   Remove skillet from oven and heat broiler to high.

7   Sprinkle remaining ½ cup cheese over top of frittata, then broil 2–4 minutes until cheese is melted and turning golden on top.

8   To serve, slice frittata into six pieces. Place one slice on each plate. Serve hot or at room temperature.

HIGH-ENERGY PROTEIN PLATES
The Sims 4

If you've got a long day ahead of being a Superstar Athlete or maybe just a big day studying at Britechester University, you may need to make a High-Energy Protein Plate. This is the type of meal that will leave you feeling energized and keep you going all day long. You can make it vegetarian by swapping the steak for 1 16-ounce block tofu, patted dry, cut into 1" cubes, and marinated in ¼ cup soy sauce, 2 tablespoons apple cider or rice wine vinegar, 2 tablespoons maple syrup, and 1 clove finely minced garlic for at least 1 hour or overnight. Drain marinade before cooking. Bake the tofu with the asparagus for 10–11 minutes at 375°F.

Serves:	Prep Time:	Cook Time:
4	10 minutes	25 minutes

8 large eggs

1 (16-ounce) sirloin steak, about 1" thick

1 tablespoon vegetable oil, divided

1½ teaspoons steak seasoning, divided

1 pound asparagus, tough ends trimmed, cut into thirds

1 Preheat broiler to high and cover a rimmed sheet pan with aluminum foil. Grease with nonstick cooking spray and place in oven.

2 In a medium pot, add eggs and fill pot with cold water until eggs are covered by 1". Place pot over high heat and bring to a rolling boil. Turn off heat and cover pot with lid. Let pot stand 3 minutes for soft-boiled eggs, 7 minutes for medium-boiled eggs, or 12 minutes for hard-boiled eggs.

3 Once eggs are cooked to your preference, carefully pour water from pan and run eggs under cool water to stop cooking. Peel and set aside.

4 Brush steak on both sides with 1½ teaspoons oil. Season on both sides with 1 teaspoon steak seasoning. Set aside.

5 Drizzle asparagus with remaining ½ tablespoon oil and toss to coat, then season with remaining ½ teaspoon steak seasoning. Set aside.

6   Once broiler is hot, place steak on prepared sheet pan and broil 5 minutes. Turn steak, move to one side of pan, and add asparagus to other side. Roast for 5–6 minutes more until asparagus is tender. Steak will be medium rare. If you want to cook steak longer, remove asparagus and broil to preferred doneness. Remove from oven and rest 3 minutes.

7   To serve, slice steak into ½"-thick slices. Divide onto four plates. Serve with asparagus and boiled eggs on the side.

Did You Know?

There are several emotional meals in *The Sims 4* that can only be created if your Sims are feeling a certain way. For example, for a Sims to eat a High-Energy Protein Plate, the Sims doing the cooking will need to be feeling energized. There are also items like Flirty Heart Cookies or Silly Gummy Bear Pancakes that can only be produced when a Sims is feeling certain emotions.

BANANA PANCAKES
The Sims 3

Picture this: It's a chilly Winterfest morning at the Pancakes' residence. Everyone's bestie, Eliza, is upstairs getting ready to open the dozens of gifts she's bound to receive, while Bob makes a delicious serving of Banana Pancakes for breakfast. Leftover pancakes can be cooled to room temperature and stored in a resealable bag in the refrigerator. To reheat, place on a microwave-safe plate and heat on high for 30–40 seconds or until pancakes are steamy hot.

Serves:	Prep Time:	Cook Time:
4	10 minutes	20 minutes

2 cups baking mix,
  such as Bisquick Pancake
  and Baking Mix

½ teaspoon baking soda

¼ teaspoon ground cinnamon

1 cup whole milk

2 large eggs

1 tablespoon unsalted butter,
  melted and cooled

1 teaspoon pure vanilla extract

2 tablespoons vegetable oil

4 medium bananas, peeled and
  sliced

4 tablespoons unsalted butter

1 cup pancake syrup

1 Preheat oven to 170°F and place a metal cooling rack on a baking sheet in oven to warm.

2 In a medium bowl, whisk together baking mix, baking soda, and cinnamon.

3 In a separate medium bowl, whisk together milk, eggs, melted butter, and vanilla. Pour wet ingredients into dry ingredients and stir until well mixed and no lumps remain. Set aside.

4 Heat a medium nonstick skillet over medium heat. Once hot, dip a paper towel into oil and lightly coat bottom of pan. Use a lightly greased ⅓-cup measuring cup to pour 2–3 pancakes into skillet. Cook 30 seconds, then gently press four banana slices on top of each pancake. Cook 1 minute or until pancake edges appear dry, some bubbles have started to form on top, and bottom of pancake is golden brown.

5 Flip pancakes and cook 60–70 seconds until other side is golden brown and pancake springs back when gently pressed in center. Transfer cooked pancakes to prepared baking sheet and keep warm in oven while you repeat with remaining batter and banana slices.

6 To serve, stack two pancakes on each plate. Top each stack with 1 tablespoon butter and ¼ cup syrup. Garnish with remaining banana slices. Serve immediately.

Special Requirements

When playing *The Sims 3*, you won't find Banana Pancakes as an obvious option for breakfast. Your Sims are going to need to get their hands on bananas, either through grocery shopping or gardening, before they are able to create specific pancake types (this is true for many of the fruits in-game).

EGGS MACHIAVELLIAN
The Sims 3

Who would've thought that some delicious watermelon would make a perfect complement to your morning eggs? This breakfast is a great choice for when you want something light that won't take too much time to cook—so you can get back to increasing your **video gaming** skill.

Serves:	Prep Time:	Cook Time:
4	5 minutes	20 minutes

12 (1"-thick) wedges watermelon

2 tablespoons vegetable oil, divided

½ teaspoon salt, divided

8 large eggs

8 ounces sliced breakfast ham

¼ teaspoon ground black pepper

2–3 dashes (⅛ teaspoon each) hot sauce, optional

1 Pat watermelon slices dry with paper towel.

2 In a medium nonstick skillet over medium heat, add 1 tablespoon oil. Once hot, add watermelon and cook 3–5 minutes per side until watermelon is slightly charred on edges. Transfer to a large plate and sprinkle with ¼ teaspoon salt. Set aside.

3 Clean out skillet and return to medium heat. Add ½ tablespoon oil and, once hot, crack in 4 eggs. Cook until whites are just set, about 2 minutes. Flip eggs and cook 1–2 minutes more until eggs are cooked to your liking. Transfer eggs to a large plate and repeat cooking with remaining ½ tablespoon oil and 4 eggs.

4 Add ham to skillet used for eggs and cook 30–40 seconds per side until hot. Remove from heat.

5 To serve: Place 2 eggs, 3 watermelon wedges, and 2 ounces of ham on each plate. Season eggs with remaining ¼ teaspoon salt, pepper, and hot sauce, if desired. Serve immediately.

Playing The Sims in The Sims
The Sims often uses previous games for the current generation. For example, when your Sims are watching TV, they are often watching things from *The Sims 3*.

EGGS BENEDICT

The Sims 4

If you're looking to impress someone with your breakfast-cooking prowess, this Eggs Benedict dish is the way to go. This meal has every breakfast ingredient you love to see, like English muffins, eggs, and the most delicious of all the bacons: Canadian bacon! It's a perfect meal on a Sunday before you head out to Magnolia Promenade for some shopping. You can use a hollandaise sauce mix purchased at the store to save time.

Serves:	Prep Time:	Cook Time:
4	10 minutes	20 minutes

1 teaspoon white vinegar

4 large eggs

4 slices Canadian bacon

3 large egg yolks

⅛ teaspoon salt

⅛ teaspoon ground black pepper

1 tablespoon lemon juice

½ cup unsalted butter, cubed

2 plain English muffins, split in half and toasted

1 tablespoon fresh chives, chopped

1 Fill a 2-quart pot with water up to 2" of pot. Stir in vinegar. Heat water over medium heat until it comes to a gentle boil, then reduce to medium-low until it cools to a simmer. Look for small bubbles gently rising to surface of water.

2 Crack eggs one at a time into a small cup. Carefully slide eggs into simmering water by touching edge of cup to the water's surface and tilting to gently release egg. Cook 2 minutes for a very runny yolk, 3 minutes for a slightly set yolk with a runny center, and 4 minutes for a fully set yolk. Use a slotted spoon to remove eggs and transfer to a paper towel–lined plate. Blot off any excess water. Set aside in a draft-free place.

3 In a small skillet over medium heat, add Canadian bacon. Cook 30 seconds per side. Turn off heat and leave in pan to keep warm.

4 In a blender, add egg yolks, salt, pepper, and lemon juice. Blend about 20 seconds, then set aside.

5 In a small saucepan, add butter and melt over medium heat until hot and foamy, about 2 minutes.

6   Slowly drizzle hot butter in a thin stream into blender until all butter is used, about 1 minute.

7   To assemble, place English muffins on a plate cut-side up, and top with 1 slice Canadian bacon, 1 egg, and hollandaise. Garnish with chives. Serve immediately.

A Special Child

In *The Sims 4*, if your Sim has a baby with Father Winter, that child will receive a Father Winter's Baby trait. This trait is awesome because it gives a kid the benefit of getting 50 percent more satisfaction points from completing **whims**. This will allow you to purchase more items from the Reward Store for your Sims.

WAFFLES
The Sims 3

Possibly Bob Pancakes' least-favorite meal, waffles are a great option for breakfast and can be totally personalized to whatever toppings you're feeling that day. Want something sweet? Go for whipped cream and fruit. Want something savory? Add some sausages on the side with maple syrup. Truly a breakfast you'll be craving every day.

Serves:	Prep Time:	Cook Time:
4	10 minutes	20 minutes

2 cups baking mix, such as Bisquick Pancake and Baking Mix

¼ teaspoon baking soda

1⅓ cups buttermilk

1 large egg

2 tablespoons unsalted butter, melted and cooled

1 teaspoon pure vanilla extract

4 tablespoons unsalted butter

1 cup pancake syrup

1   Preheat oven to 170°F and place a metal cooling rack on a baking sheet in oven to warm.

2   Preheat waffle iron. Once hot, lightly grease with nonstick cooking spray.

3   In a medium bowl, whisk together baking mix and baking soda.

4   In a separate medium bowl, whisk together buttermilk, egg, melted butter, and vanilla. Pour wet ingredients into dry ingredients and stir until well mixed and no lumps remain. Set aside.

5   Pour batter into center of waffle iron based on manufacturer's recommended amount. Bake until there is no steam coming from waffle iron and waffles are golden brown and firm, about 4–5 minutes.

6   Transfer cooked waffle to prepared baking sheet and keep warm in oven while you repeat cooking with remaining batter.

7 To serve, divide waffles on four plates. Top each serving with 1 tablespoon butter and drizzle with ¼ cup syrup. Serve immediately.

Check Your Waffle Iron

Waffle irons differ in size and volume, so be sure to read the instructions for your waffle iron to determine how much batter to add. Smaller waffle irons, like mini-waffle makers, use ¼ cup, but larger family-sized waffle makers may take ¾–1 cup of batter. Larger waffles may need to be divided to achieve the recommended serving amount in this recipe.

FRUIT AND YOGURT PARFAIT
The Sims 3 and *The Sims 4*

If you're looking for an extremely simple, no-cooking-required breakfast option, this Fruit and Yogurt Parfait is an incredible choice. You can add your favorite toppings and completely customize it to your liking; think of it like creating a Sim...but with yogurt. Just don't add eyelashes; that would be weird.

Serves:	Prep Time:	Cook Time:
1	5 minutes	N/A

6 ounces vanilla yogurt

¼ cup granola

¼ cup fresh blueberries

¼ cup hulled and sliced fresh strawberries

1 teaspoon amber honey

1 sprig fresh mint

In a bowl, add half the yogurt. Layer with half granola, half blueberries, and half strawberries. Top with remaining yogurt. Sprinkle remaining granola over top, then drizzle with honey. Place remaining blueberries in center of yogurt, then arrange reserved strawberry slices around blueberries. Garnish with mint. Serve immediately.

OMELET

The Sims 2, The Sims 3, and *The Sims 4*

If you're running low on ingredients and haven't had a chance to grab more groceries, this Omelet is a way healthier option than ordering yourself some Zoomers food delivery. Omelets are great because you can use whatever is in your fridge!

Serves:	Prep Time:	Cook Time:
1	10 minutes	10 minutes

1 tablespoon unsalted butter

3 large eggs

⅛ teaspoon salt

⅛ teaspoon ground black pepper

¼ cup shredded sharp
    Cheddar cheese

¼ cup chopped ham

3 cherry tomatoes, quartered

1 tablespoon plus 1 teaspoon
    fresh chopped chives,
    divided

1 In an 8" nonstick skillet over medium heat, add butter. Let melt.

2 In a medium bowl, add eggs and whisk until well combined. Add salt and pepper and whisk to combine.

3 Once butter is melted and starts to foam, about 30 seconds, add eggs. Let pan stand 20 seconds or until eggs start to set, then reduce heat to low.

4 Using a silicone or heatproof spatula, gently push edges of eggs to center of pan while tilting so uncooked eggs move to edges, about 2 minutes.

5 Once bottom of eggs are just set and top is still slightly wet, add cheese, ham, tomatoes, and 1 tablespoon chives.

6 Remove pan from heat and fold top ⅓ of omelet down, then fold in half. Transfer to a dinner plate. Garnish with remaining 1 teaspoon chives and serve.

Totally Customizable

One of the best things about making an omelet for breakfast is the ability to turn it into whatever you want. You can really use any fillings in this recipe, including bacon, sausage, and even a mix of sautéed vegetables for a different experience each time. You can also mix up the types of cheese you use to add different flavors!

CHAPTER TWO
LUNCH

Lunch is one of those meals that really helps get a person through a busy day. It's something to look forward to when working long hours at the Secret Lab and trying to protect an entire town from a mysterious illness—and it's definitely the best part of a child's day at Landgraab Elementary.

However, coming up with interesting options for lunch is one hard task, especially when you just don't have the time. That's why this chapter is filled with tried and tested lunch recipes that are delicious and bring back memories of playing The Sims. You'll find a variety of dishes that can be prepared quickly and a few that take a bit more time for your days off or when you do have some time to spare. These recipes include traditional Grilled Cheese (a staple in The Sims), Chef's Salad, Salmon Maki Rolls, and so much more.

GRILLED CHEESE
The Sims 2, The Sims 3, and *The Sims 4*

Oh, grilled cheese. A staple of The Sims franchise since *The Sims 2*, and a staple of childhoods for decades. This meal pairs perfectly with a bowl of delicious tomato soup; just make sure Vlad understands that it's soup and not his next meal. If you don't want American cheese, Swiss and Muenster, Cheddar and Swiss, or Havarti and Monterey jack are all tasty pairings. For a spicy kick, try pepper jack cheese!

Serves:	Prep Time:	Cook Time:
4	7 minutes	8 minutes

3 tablespoons unsalted butter, softened, divided

8 slices white sandwich bread

4 slices American cheese

4 slices medium Cheddar cheese

1 Heat a large nonstick pan over medium heat. Add 1½ tablespoons butter. Once butter starts to foam, about 30 seconds, swirl pan to evenly coat, then add 4 slices bread. Top each slice with 1 slice each American and Cheddar.

2 Butter remaining 4 slices bread with remaining 1½ tablespoons butter and place butter-side up on top of cheese. Cook 2–3 minutes per side until each side is crisp and golden brown.

3 Transfer to four plates and cool 2 minutes before enjoying.

Did You Know?
Did you know that there's an entire secret aspiration surrounding grilled cheese in *The Sims 4*? Yup! Just have your Sim eat three grilled cheese sandwiches in a row, and a notification will appear letting you know you've unlocked a new aspiration. You'll need to complete things like eating a grilled cheese in space and talking to the Grim Reaper about grilled cheese.

MONTE CRISTO SANDWICHES
The Sims 4

If you're looking for a twist on the regular lunch sandwich and have a bit of extra time, you should definitely try a Monte Cristo. This sandwich is crispy on the outside and warm and gooey on the inside. And when you dip it in some raspberry jam, you'll be trying flavors you never thought should go together—but they do!

Serves:	Prep Time:	Cook Time:
4	5 minutes	10 minutes

½ cup whole milk

2 large eggs

8 slices sandwich bread

4 slices Swiss cheese

8 slices thin-cut deli honey ham

8 slices thin-cut deli roasted turkey breast

4 slices Cheddar cheese

3 tablespoons unsalted butter

¼ cup confectioners' sugar

1 cup seedless raspberry jam

1. In a medium bowl, whisk together milk and eggs. Set aside.

2. Top each of 4 bread slices with 1 slice Swiss, 2 slices ham, 2 slices turkey, and 1 slice Cheddar. Top with remaining bread.

3. Heat a large nonstick skillet or griddle over medium heat and add butter. Once melted, tilt pan or griddle to evenly coat.

4. Dip sandwiches into egg mixture, making sure both sides are evenly coated, until bread is well soaked but not soggy. Place sandwiches onto prepared skillet and cook 3–5 minutes until golden brown.

5. Flip sandwich and cook 3–5 minutes until golden brown on other side and cheese is melted. If cheese is not melted, turn heat to low and continue to cook, flipping sandwich every 30 seconds until cheese is melted.

Continued on next page

6 Remove from heat and let cool 1 minute before serving. To serve, slice sandwiches into triangles and arrange on a serving platter. Dust with sugar and serve with jam on the side for dipping. Serve warm.

Creating a Perfect Sandwich

Honey ham and roasted turkey are mild in flavor and are well balanced with the cheese, eggy bread, and jam, but smoked ham and turkey can be used if desired. Any berry jam can be used here, but it should be seedless. Another note: Less is more when it comes to this sandwich. Loading it with lots of extra meat and cheese means the center of the sandwich will not heat through while cooking.

SPINACH-WRAPPED VEGGIE BURRITOS

The Sims 4: City Living

A Spinach-Wrapped Veggie Burrito is an awesome vegetarian option for keeping you full until dinner. This will definitely help you get all your veggies in—without turning into the Flower Bunny from eating too many carrots.

Serves:	Prep Time:	Cook Time:
4	15 minutes	10 minutes

½ cup fire-roasted corn kernels, canned or frozen and thawed

1 medium Roma tomato, seeded and diced

2 tablespoons minced onion

1 tablespoon minced fresh cilantro

1 teaspoon lime juice

⅛ teaspoon salt

4 (12″) spinach wraps

1 cup vegetarian refried black beans

1 pouch Ben's Original Ready Rice Cilantro Lime, or 1 cup cooked rice

½ cup mashed avocado

1. In a small bowl, combine corn, tomato, onion, cilantro, lime juice, and salt. Set aside.

2. Heat a griddle pan over medium heat. Place a wrap on heated griddle and cook for 20 seconds per side or until warm and soft. Transfer to a large plate and cover with a towel while you heat remaining wraps.

3. Heat beans in a small microwave-safe bowl on high in microwave 30 seconds. Stir, then return to microwave for 20 seconds. Stir well and set aside.

4. Prepare rice according to package directions.

5. To assemble, spread ¼ cup beans over center of each wrap. Top with rice, avocado, and prepared corn mixture.

6. Fold up bottom of wrap, fold in sides, then roll up. Serve immediately.

Grilled to Perfection

If you're a fan of melted cheese, grill your burrito! Add your favorite cheese to this recipe, then place your burrito *seam-side down* onto a griddle over medium heat until golden, roll it over, and toast the other side until the cheese inside melts.

CHEF'S SALAD
The Sims 2

You definitely don't have to be a **master chef** to make this delicious Chef's Salad (but it doesn't hurt). This salad is fresh and flavorful, providing the perfect level of crunch to balance the softer ingredients like deli turkey and ham. It will keep you full for hours so you can head over to Magnolia Blossom Park for your big date with Johnny Zest.

Serves:	Prep Time:	Cook Time:
4	1 hour 20 minutes	N/A

1 medium head Boston lettuce, trimmed and torn into bite-sized pieces

1 medium head iceberg lettuce, trimmed and torn into bite-sized pieces

4 large hard-boiled eggs, sliced

⅓ medium English cucumber, sliced thin

½ medium green bell pepper, cored, seeded, and chopped

3 slices Swiss cheese, cut into matchstick pieces

¼ pound thick-cut deli roasted turkey breast, chopped

¼ pound thick-cut deli Black Forest ham, chopped

16 cherry tomatoes, sliced in half

16 pitted black olives, sliced in half

1 cup salad dressing of your choice, such as ranch, blue cheese, or honey mustard

1 Place lettuce in a large serving bowl. Arrange eggs, cucumbers, bell pepper, cheese, turkey, ham, tomatoes, and olives over lettuce. Cover and refrigerate 1 hour.

2 To serve, toss salad with dressing and serve immediately.

Always Wash Your Greens

Bagged salad greens can be used in place of the lettuce. Aim for 1½ pounds of salad greens. Always wash bagged greens, even if the label says they are already washed.

SUPERFOOD SALAD

The Sims 4: Spa Day

If you're starting to focus on your personal **wellness** you should definitely try making this Superfood Salad. Filled with awesome nutrients and supergreens, this recipe will not disappoint. Unlocked in-game at level 4 of the **wellness** skill, you and your Sims will leave this meal feeling refreshed and full. What more could you want?

Serves:	Prep Time:	Cook Time:
4	20 minutes	N/A

3 cups fresh baby spinach

2 cups chopped kale

½ cup canned black beans, drained and rinsed

½ cup mandarin orange slices

½ cup cherry tomatoes, cut in half

½ cup pumpkin seeds

½ cup chopped walnuts

½ cup pomegranate seeds

1 medium avocado, pitted, peeled, and sliced

¼ cup extra-virgin olive oil

2 tablespoons lemon juice

1 teaspoon Dijon mustard

1 teaspoon pure maple syrup

¼ teaspoon salt

¼ teaspoon ground black pepper

1   In a large salad bowl, combine spinach, kale, beans, orange slices, tomatoes, pumpkin seeds, walnuts, and pomegranate seeds. Top salad with avocado slices.

2   In a small bowl, whisk together oil, lemon juice, mustard, maple syrup, salt, and pepper. Drizzle salad with dressing and serve immediately.

Meditation or Teleportation?

If you get a Sim in *The Sims 4: Spa Day* to get their **wellness** skill to level 10 and they've previously traveled to the hidden worlds of Sylvan Glade or Forgotten Grotto, they are able to use the meditation stools to teleport straight to these locations. Definitely saves you some time and just looks superfun!

MAC AND CHEESE
The Sims 2, The Sims 3, and The Sims 4

Perhaps the most comforting dish you can cook in the world, both real and virtual. Mac and Cheese is great for those days when you work too hard and need to feel something warm in your tummy. Cook it on the stove or in a cauldron; either way, this meal is delicious! Just be sure to make enough for the whole family.

Serves:	Prep Time:	Cook Time:
2	10 minutes	12 minutes

1¼ teaspoons salt, divided

8 ounces dry elbow pasta

1 tablespoon salted butter

⅔ cup (6 ounces) evaporated milk

1 large egg, beaten

1 teaspoon dry mustard

1 cup shredded medium Cheddar cheese

¼ teaspoon fresh cracked black pepper

4 dashes (½ teaspoon) hot sauce

1 Fill a medium pot with 2 quarts water and add 1 teaspoon salt. Bring to a rolling boil over high heat, then add pasta. Cook 7 minutes, stirring often. Strain pasta and return to pot.

2 Reduce heat to medium-low and add butter. Stir until butter is melted and coats pasta.

3 In a medium bowl, whisk together milk, egg, and dry mustard. Add mixture to pasta and cook, stirring constantly, until milk mixture thickens, about 5 minutes.

4 Remove pot from heat and add cheese. Stir until cheese is melted and smooth, then add remaining ¼ teaspoon salt, pepper, and hot sauce. Serve immediately.

Did You Know?
In *The Sims 4: Realm of Magic*, your Sims are actually able to cook Mac and Cheese inside of a cauldron. This way of cooking is great for Spellcasters who maybe just don't want a stove or are too busy learning magic to cook for their kids, since cauldron foods last a bit longer than food sitting on a countertop.

AUTUMN SALAD
The Sims 3

The perfect salad to eat during those months when the leaves are changing and shorts are no longer appropriate. Of course, townies in The Sims wear what they want, when they want. Hello, eyeball ring! This salad can be prepared in advance before it is dressed and stored in the refrigerator until ready to serve, up to 1 day.

Serves:	Prep Time:	Cook Time:
4	20 minutes	4 minutes

1 small eggplant, trimmed and cut into ¼"-thick slices

1 medium head romaine lettuce, trimmed and chopped

½ medium head iceberg lettuce, trimmed and chopped

1 medium green bell pepper, cored, seeded, and thinly sliced

½ medium red onion, peeled and sliced

1 pint cherry tomatoes, cut in half

¼ cup extra-virgin olive oil

2 tablespoons balsamic vinegar

1 teaspoon Dijon mustard

1 teaspoon amber honey

¼ teaspoon salt

¼ teaspoon ground black pepper

1 Heat a grill pan over medium heat and grease lightly with nonstick cooking spray. Once hot, grill eggplant slices 2 minutes per side or until tender and slightly charred. Set aside to cool.

2 Place lettuce in a large serving bowl along with cooled eggplant, bell pepper, onion, and tomatoes.

3 In a small bowl, whisk together oil, vinegar, mustard, honey, salt, and black pepper.

4 To serve, toss salad with dressing and serve immediately.

Don't Forget to Grill
Eggplant can be tricky when you're adding it to salads. When raw, it is pretty bitter and will ruin the overall taste of your Autumn Salad, so it's important to grill it first to make the flavor less bitter. You can even go ahead and add a sliced apple to this recipe right before serving for an extra crunch and delicious flavor!

PASTA PRIMAVERA
The Sims 4

If you can't decide between a salad or carbs, this Pasta Primavera is an incredible option that won't leave you feeling too heavy. This pasta dish features all sorts of vegetables that make it taste fresh while still giving you that comfort food feeling you want from a pasta dish.

Serves:	Prep Time:	Cook Time:
4	20 minutes	15 minutes

1 teaspoon salt

8 ounces dry penne pasta

3 tablespoons olive oil

½ medium yellow onion, peeled and sliced

1 medium red bell pepper, cored, seeded, and sliced

1 medium zucchini, trimmed and sliced

1 medium yellow squash, trimmed and sliced

2 cloves garlic, peeled and minced

1 cup cherry tomatoes, sliced in half

½ teaspoon Italian seasoning

½ teaspoon flaky sea salt

¼ teaspoon ground black pepper

4 fresh basil leaves, torn into small pieces

¼ cup fresh grated Parmesan cheese

1   Fill a large pot with 6 quarts water and add salt. Bring to a rolling boil over high heat, then add pasta. Cook, stirring occasionally, until pasta is tender, about 8 minutes. Reserve ½ cup of pasta water, then drain pasta and set aside.

2   In a large skillet over medium heat, add oil. Once hot, add onion and cook 1 minute or until just tender. Add bell pepper and cook 1 minute or until starting to soften, then add zucchini, squash, and garlic. Cook, stirring often, until all vegetables are tender, 3–5 minutes.

3   Add pasta, ¼ cup reserved pasta water, tomatoes, Italian seasoning, salt, and black pepper. Cook, stirring constantly, until pasta is hot and well combined with vegetables, about 30 seconds. If you need to loosen sauce, add additional pasta water a tablespoon at a time until consistency is to your liking.

4   To serve, transfer pasta to a serving platter. Garnish with basil and cheese. Serve immediately.

GARLIC NOODLES
The Sims 4

Garlic Noodles are extremely delicious, and this meal is great for scaring away any Vampires who might come to your door at night. (You may want to pick a different meal before attending the Romance Festival, however.) Sprinkle a little cheese on top for extra deliciousness!

Serves:	Prep Time:	Cook Time:
4	5 minutes	11 minutes

1 teaspoon salt

12 ounces dry lo mein noodles

8 tablespoons unsalted butter

6 cloves garlic, peeled and minced

2 tablespoons oyster sauce

1 tablespoon soy sauce

1 teaspoon packed light brown sugar

1 teaspoon toasted sesame oil

1 medium green onion, chopped

1 tablespoon toasted sesame seeds

1   Fill a large pot with 6 quarts water and add salt. Bring to a boil over high heat, then add noodles. Boil, stirring occasionally, until tender, 4–6 minutes. Drain well and rinse under cold water to stop cooking. Set aside.

2   In a large skillet or wok over medium heat, add butter. Once melted, add garlic and stir-fry until lightly golden in color, about 4 minutes. Stir in oyster sauce, soy sauce, sugar, and oil and mix well.

3   Add cooked noodles and toss to coat until noodles are heated through, about 1 minute, then add green onion and toss to mix.

4   Transfer noodles to a large plate and garnish with sesame seeds. Serve.

SALMON MAKI ROLL
The Sims 4

Buying sushi can get expensive quickly, especially without an IRL **motherlode** cheat. Making a Salmon Maki Roll at home is simple, affordable, and delicious. Sushi-grade fish is imperative here, so be sure to go to a trusted fishmonger or a Japanese/Korean/Asian market to source this. If it is not available, you can use strips of seared salmon or cured/cold smoked salmon.

Serves:	Prep Time:	Cook Time:
4	20 minutes	15 minutes

1 cup short-grain rice

1 cup water

1 tablespoon sushi vinegar

½ teaspoon salt

4 sheets nori

2 ounces sushi-grade salmon cut for sashimi

3 tablespoons gari (Japanese pickled ginger)

4 teaspoons prepared wasabi

1   Add rice to a large bowl. Cover with cool water and swirl rice with a spoon for 20 seconds. Repeat three times or until water from rice is mostly clear.

2   Place rice and water into a medium saucepan. Bring to boil over high heat, then cover, reduce heat to low, and cook 15 minutes.

3   Once rice is done, remove from heat and let stand, covered, for 10 minutes.

4   Once rice has rested, heat vinegar and salt in a small microwave-safe bowl in microwave on high 15 seconds or until steaming hot and salt is dissolved.

5   Transfer cooked rice to a large glass or wood bowl and add heated vinegar. Gently fold in rice to coat all grains in vinegar, being careful not to smash rice. Let rice cool to room temperature, about 30 minutes.

6   Place a sheet of plastic wrap on a work surface and top with a sheet of nori, rough-side up. Spread ¼ of rice mixture over nori, leaving ½" strip at end of nori sheet closest to you.

Continued on next page

7　Place strip of salmon 1" from top edge of nori. Roll nori toward you, using plastic wrap to help press and shape the roll as you go. Cut roll in half, then cut each half into three pieces. Repeat with remaining nori, rice, and salmon.

8　Serve immediately with gari and wasabi on the side, or cover and refrigerate up to 4 hours before serving.

Can't Find Sushi Vinegar?

Sushi vinegar is commonly found in most grocery stores and has a tangy, sweet taste. If it is unavailable, you can use 1 tablespoon rice vinegar mixed with 1 teaspoon sugar.

SAUSAGE AND PEPPERS
The Sims 4: Luxury Party Stuff

Sometimes you need to feel something from food and get some **happy** moodlets going after you eat it. And honestly, this Sausage and Peppers dish can make you feel those warm fuzzies. This recipe requires just a few simple ingredients and barely any prep time before you can chow down. It can even be cooked outside on a grill or open fire when hanging out in Granite Falls!

Serves:	Prep Time:	Cook Time:
4	10 minutes	12 minutes

1 medium red bell pepper, cored, seeded, and cut into 1" strips

1 medium yellow bell pepper, cored, seeded, and cut into 1" strips

1 tablespoon olive oil

¼ teaspoon steak seasoning

4 fully cooked sausage links of your choice, such as Johnsonville or Aidells

1 Add peppers to a large bowl along with oil and seasoning. Toss well to coat. Set aside.

2 Heat grill or grill pan to medium heat. Once hot, lightly grease grate with nonstick cooking spray or use tongs to wipe with a paper towel lightly coated with oil. Add sausages and pepper strips to grill. If cooking on an outdoor grill, use a grill basket or foil basket for peppers to prevent them from falling through grill grate.

3 Grill sausages 2–3 minutes per side until sausages have grill marks and reach an internal temperature of 160°F. Cook peppers, turning often, until lightly charred and tender, about 5 minutes.

4 Transfer to a serving platter and serve hot.

SHISH KEBABS
The Sims 4: Outdoor Retreat

Shish Kebabs are a fun meal to prepare as a family; even kids can join in and help put things on the skewers! Since these Shish Kebabs came to The Sims with *Outdoor Retreat*, it's only fair that you bring a serving of these to the Hermit in the woods: Who knows when they last had a good meal? Just be sure to watch your back, you never know what weird stuff they might be getting up to out there.

Serves:	Prep Time:	Cook Time:
4	50 minutes	6 minutes

1 pound beef sirloin or strip steak, cut into 1" cubes (for medium steak)

2 tablespoons olive oil

2 tablespoons soy sauce

1 tablespoon Dijon mustard

1 teaspoon Worcestershire sauce

1 teaspoon lemon juice

½ teaspoon steak seasoning

½ medium green bell pepper, cored, seeded, and cut into 1" pieces

½ medium yellow bell pepper, cored, seeded, and cut into 1" pieces

½ medium yellow onion, peeled and cut into 1" pieces

6 cherry tomatoes

4 button mushrooms, cut in half

1   Place steak cubes in a medium bowl along with oil, soy sauce, mustard, Worcestershire, lemon juice, and seasoning. Toss to coat, cover with plastic wrap, and let stand at room temperature 30 minutes.

2   While beef marinates, soak four long wooden skewers in warm water or lightly grease metal skewers with nonstick cooking spray, then wipe away any excess.

3   To assemble, alternately thread beef with vegetables until each skewer is filled.

4   Heat grill or grill pan to medium heat. Once hot, lightly grease grate with nonstick cooking spray or use tongs to wipe with a paper towel lightly coated with oil. Add skewers and grill 2–3 minutes per side until steak is cooked to medium and vegetables are lightly charred and tender.

5   Transfer to a serving platter and serve hot.

How Do You Like Your Steak?
If you prefer the steak to be cooked medium rare, cut the cubes to be thicker, about 1½". For more well-done steak, cut it less thick, about ½".

CHAPTER THREE

DINNER

Now, this is where things get even more interesting. Dinner should fill your **hunger** need quickly and keep you feeling full for hours, but it should also be a delicious meal you look forward to.

In this chapter, you'll find some real classics like Lobster Thermidor and Grandma's Comfort Soup, as well as unique recipes like Goopy Carbonara and Stu Surprise. These dishes are soon to become your go-to meals for dinners alone, with friends, or when you really need to impress the private school Headmaster. From Chicken Saltimbocca to Hot and Sour Soup, they are sure to please even the **snobbiest** of Sims—and people, and will leave your guests coming back for more every time. So fire up your stove and get cooking, but just be sure to purchase a smoke detector first.

CHILI CON CARNE
The Sims 2 and *The Sims 3: Supernatural*

Chili con Carne seems like the perfect family meal, a meal that Mary-Sue Pleasant would cook for Daniel—but only before finding out what's been going on behind her back. Maybe next time Daniel can cook his own dinner...served best with breadsticks!

Serves:	Prep Time:	Cook Time:
4	20 minutes	1 hour 20 minutes

1 pound ground chuck

½ teaspoon salt

½ teaspoon ground black pepper

½ medium white onion, peeled and chopped

2 cloves garlic, peeled and minced

2 tablespoons chopped chipotle chile in adobo

¼ cup chili powder

1½ teaspoons ground cumin

1½ cups beef broth

2 tablespoons masa harina

¼ cup water

2 teaspoons lime juice

1 teaspoon granulated sugar

1 cup shredded sharp Cheddar cheese

½ cup sour cream

1 In a large skillet over medium heat, add beef. Cook until thoroughly browned, about 8 minutes. Drain off excess fat and return to heat.

2 Season beef with salt and pepper, then add onion and cook until onion is tender, about 5 minutes. Add garlic and cook for 1 minute.

3 Add chipotle chile, chili powder, and cumin and mix well. Add broth and scrape any bits off bottom of pan. Bring mixture to a boil over high heat, then reduce to medium-low and until mixture comes to a simmer. Cover and cook for 1 hour.

4 In a small bowl, mix masa with water and stir into chili. Increase heat to high and bring back to a boil and stir constantly until thickened, about 5 minutes. Turn off heat and stir in lime juice and sugar. Serve hot with shredded cheese and sour cream for garnish.

Fire-Breathing Sim

In *The Sims 3: Supernatural*, if you have a Sim prepare Chili con Carne or Hot and Sour Soup with a ghost chili, the Sims who consume it have a chance of literally breathing fire. Be careful, because when *Supernatural* was released, this tiny detail engulfed numerous players' homes in flames, and they lost entire dining room sets and kitchens!

STU SURPRISE
The Sims 3

When Stu Surprise arrived in *The Sims 3*, it left many players wondering exactly what was inside. What is the surprise? Unfortunately, the game only required your Sims to have two of any **ingredients** to cook the dish, so we may never know what is inside. Thankfully, this recipe *does* include every ingredient you need to prepare it! This dish is perfect for a gloomy day when all you want is to curl up and play for hours.

Serves:	Prep Time:	Cook Time:
4	20 minutes	2 hours 45 minutes

- 1½ **pounds chuck roast, cut into 1" cubes**
- ½ **cup all-purpose flour**
- 2 **tablespoons vegetable oil**
- 1 **medium white onion, peeled and chopped**
- 1 **medium celery stalk, chopped**
- 2 **cloves garlic, peeled and minced**
- 2 **tablespoons tomato paste**
- ⅓ **cup dry red wine**
- 2 **medium carrots, peeled and cut into ½" pieces**
- 2 **large russet potatoes, peeled and cut into ½" cubes**
- 1 **(2-ounce) packet French onion soup mix**
- 3 **cups water**
- 1 **bay leaf**
- ½ **teaspoon ground black pepper**

1 In a large zip-top bag, add beef and flour. Shake until beef cubes are coated in flour. Set aside.

2 In a large Dutch oven or heavy-bottom pot with lid over medium-high heat, add oil. Once hot, remove coated beef cubes from bag and shake off excess flour, then add to pot, leaving about ½" between each cube. Brown well on all sides, about 2 minutes per side. Transfer to a large plate and repeat browning with remaining beef.

3 Reduce heat to medium and add onion and celery. Cook until just tender, about 2 minutes, then add garlic and tomato paste. Cook 2 minutes or until garlic is very fragrant and tomato paste is darker in color. Add wine and scrape bottom of pan to loosen any brown bits, then let wine reduce by half, about 5 minutes.

4 Return beef to pot along with any collected juices, then add remaining ingredients. Stir well. Bring to a boil over high heat, cover with lid, leaving one side slightly vented. Reduce heat to low and let simmer for 2½ hours or until beef is fork-tender. Serve hot.

GOOPY CARBONARA

The Sims 3

After a long, hard day of killing Sims by removing the pool ladder, you deserve a warm bowl of Goopy Carbonara pasta. This meal is supereasy to make and doesn't require a ton of prep time. It's an awesome choice for weekday dinners when you'd rather just be playing with your virtual Sims family than working away in the kitchen.

Serves:	Prep Time:	Cook Time:
4	10 minutes	20 minutes

1 tablespoon olive oil

6 strips thick-cut bacon, cubed

1 clove garlic, peeled and minced

¼ cup dry white wine

3 large eggs

1 cup fresh grated Parmesan
cheese, divided

¼ cup heavy cream

½ teaspoon ground black pepper

1 teaspoon salt

1 pound dry spaghetti

1 In a large skillet over medium heat, add oil. Once hot, add bacon and cook until crisp, about 5 minutes. Transfer bacon to paper towel and pour off all but 3 tablespoons of bacon fat. Return pan to heat and add garlic and wine. Cook until reduced by half, about 4 minutes. Remove from heat.

2 In a medium bowl, beat eggs together with ½ cup cheese, cream, and pepper.

3 In a large pot, add 6 quarts water and salt. Bring to a boil over high heat and add spaghetti, ensuring that it is all submerged in water. Cook according to package directions, but reduce cooking time by 1 minute. Reserve 1 cup of pasta water, then drain pasta well.

4 Return skillet to medium heat. Once hot, add pasta and ½ cup reserved pasta water. Toss pasta so each strand is coated in sauce and pasta is steaming hot. Remove pan from heat and immediately add egg mixture while tossing to mix. If sauce seems too thick, add reserved pasta water 1 tablespoon at a time until loosened to your liking.

Continued on next page

5 To serve, transfer pasta to a serving platter. Garnish with cooked bacon and remaining ½ cup cheese. Serve immediately.

Fun Fact!
It is presumed that the dish Goopy Carbonara is named after a character in the franchise named Goopy GilsCarbo. This character appeared in *The Sims 2* as an adult and was available for purchase in *The Sims 3* store. You can even take a class in *The Sims 4: Discover University* called "Beyond Cooking Goopy Carbonara" to help your Sims learn the **cooking** skill.

CHICKEN SALTIMBOCCA
The Sims 4

After a long day of work trying to solve the StrangerVille Mystery, you'll definitely need a good serving of protein to keep you going; those **spore clusters** aren't going to collect themselves! This Chicken Saltimbocca recipe brings chicken and prosciutto together in one of the most delicious sauces known to humankind. You'll be begging to eat this every day.

Serves:	Prep Time:	Cook Time:
4	15 minutes	20 minutes

4 (4-ounce) chicken breast cutlets

½ teaspoon salt

½ teaspoon ground black pepper

8 fresh sage leaves

8 strips prosciutto

2 tablespoons all-purpose flour

2 tablespoons vegetable oil

2 tablespoons salted butter

½ medium white onion, peeled and finely chopped

2 cloves garlic, peeled and minced

½ cup dry white wine

½ cup chicken broth

2 teaspoons lemon juice

1 Season both sides of cutlets with salt and pepper. Lay 2 sage leaves on each cutlet, then wrap each cutlet in 2 slices of prosciutto. Dust each wrapped cutlet lightly with flour and set aside.

2 Heat a large skillet over medium-high heat. Add oil and, once hot, add cutlets. Cook until each side is browned and chicken is just cooked through, about 3 minutes per side. Transfer chicken to a large plate.

3 Add butter to skillet. Once melted, add onion and cook, stirring often, until tender, about 3 minutes. Add garlic and cook until fragrant, about 30 seconds. Add wine and broth, scraping bottom of pan to loosen any brown bits, and cook until reduced by half, about 5 minutes. Stir in lemon juice.

4 Return cutlets to pan and reduce heat to medium-low. Let chicken simmer until cooked through or a thermometer inserted into thickest part of breast reaches 165°F, about 5 minutes.

5 Transfer chicken to a serving platter and spoon sauce over top. Enjoy immediately.

GRANDMA'S COMFORT SOUP
The Sims 2: Freetime

If you've got a case of Itchy Plumbob or the Llama Flu, you definitely need to try a bowl of Grandma's Comfort Soup. This soup will get you off the couch and feeling great in no time; however, if your grandma is Agnes Crumplebottom, you probably shouldn't grab candies from the bottom of her purse again, as that's likely how you got sick in the first place. Swap the diced chicken for shredded if preferred.

Serves:	Prep Time:	Cook Time:
6	10 minutes	15 minutes

1 tablespoon salted butter

1 medium yellow onion, peeled and chopped

2 medium stalks celery, chopped

1 medium carrot, peeled and chopped

½ teaspoon poultry seasoning

¼ teaspoon salt

¼ teaspoon ground black pepper

1 bay leaf

8 cups chicken stock

8 ounces dry wide egg noodles

2 cups diced cooked chicken

1 tablespoon lemon juice

1 In a large pot with a lid over medium heat, add butter. Once hot, add onion, celery, and carrot. Cook until just tender, about 3 minutes. Add poultry seasoning, salt, pepper, and bay leaf and stir well. Add stock, and once it comes to a boil, add noodles. Cook until noodles are tender, about 10 minutes.

2 Stir in chicken and lemon juice. Cook until chicken is heated through, about 2 minutes. Serve hot.

TUNA CASSEROLE
The Sims 4

Tuna Casserole is one of those dishes reminiscent of Mom's home cooking. Can't you just picture Mila Munch cooking a delicious Tuna Casserole for her three boys? This is definitely a comfort dish that you won't want to skip.

Serves:	Prep Time:	Cook Time:
6	20 minutes	40 minutes

4 ounces dry medium-width egg noodles

1 (10-ounce) can condensed cream of mushroom soup

½ cup whole milk

1 cup shredded mild Cheddar cheese

½ cup frozen green peas

2 (5-ounce) cans chunk light tuna in water, drained well

½ cup crushed kettle-cooked potato chips

1 tablespoon unsalted butter, melted

¼ cup finely chopped fresh parsley

1 Cook noodles according to package directions, shortening cooking time by 2 minutes. Drain and rinse under cool water to stop cooking.

2 Preheat oven to 375°F and grease a 2-quart casserole dish with nonstick cooking spray.

3 In a large bowl, add soup and milk. Whisk until smooth, then add noodles, cheese, peas, and tuna. Combine.

4 Transfer tuna mixture to prepared casserole dish. Bake 20 minutes.

5 While casserole bakes, combine potato chips and butter in a medium bowl.

6 Once casserole has baked, spread chips over top. Bake 10–12 minutes until chips are golden brown and casserole is bubbling.

7 Let casserole cool 10 minutes before garnishing with parsley and serving.

Alternatives to Peas
You can omit the peas and add any chopped and sautéed veggies you prefer. A combination of chopped onion and celery (¼ cup of each) or ½ cup bell peppers (any mix of red, yellow, or green) would be nice here.

CIOPPINO

The Sims 4

Are you a Sim with a high **fishing** skill? Are you looking to improve your **cooking** skill? Look no further! Those two skills mesh perfectly when cooking Cioppino. This fish stew takes whatever seafood you have on hand and turns it into a hearty meal perfect for sharing with friends and family. (Just avoid fatty fish like salmon, which can make the soup greasy.)

Serves:	Prep Time:	Cook Time:
6	20 minutes	37 minutes

3 tablespoons light olive oil

1 medium yellow onion, peeled and chopped

1 medium red bell pepper, cored, seeded, and chopped

2 cloves garlic, peeled and minced

1 (28-ounce) can crushed tomatoes

1 cup dry red wine

1 cup seafood stock

1 tablespoon lemon juice

1 bay leaf

¼ cup chopped fresh basil

½ teaspoon ground black pepper

1 pound fresh mussels, scrubbed and beards removed

1 pound peeled and deveined uncooked large shrimp

1 pound clams, scrubbed

1 In a large pot with a lid over medium heat, add oil. Once hot, add onion and bell pepper. Cook until just tender, about 3 minutes. Add garlic and cook until fragrant, about 30 seconds. Add tomatoes, wine, stock, lemon juice, bay leaf, basil, and black pepper. Stir well, then increase heat to high and bring to a boil. Once boiling, close lid, reduce heat to medium-low, and let simmer 30 minutes.

2 Remove lid and stir well. Remove bay leaf and add mussels, shrimp, and clams. Increase heat to medium and cook until shrimp are pink and shellfish have opened, about 3 minutes. Serve hot.

LOBSTER THERMIDOR
The Sims 2, The Sims 3, and The Sims 4

Lobster Thermidor is possibly the best dish for impressing the private school Headmaster. Serve for dinner, then enjoy a delicious Baked Alaska for dessert. Your kids will definitely be wearing uniforms on their next school day.

Serves:	Prep Time:	Cook Time:
4	20 minutes	16 minutes

2 teaspoons salt

4 (8-ounce) fresh lobster tails

2 tablespoons unsalted butter

2 tablespoons vegetable oil

½ medium white onion, peeled and finely chopped

2 cloves garlic, peeled and minced

2 tablespoons all-purpose flour

2 tablespoons brandy or white wine

½ cup half-and-half

¼ teaspoon dry tarragon

¼ teaspoon salt

¼ teaspoon ground black pepper

¼ cup plus 2 tablespoons Parmesan cheese, divided

¼ cup fine plain bread crumbs

1 teaspoon olive oil

¼ cup chopped fresh parsley

1   Fill a large pot with 6 cups water and add salt. Bring to a boil over high heat, then add lobster tails and cook 7 minutes.

2   Once cooked, drain and rinse tails with cold water to stop cooking. With sharp kitchen shears, cut away underside of shells. Remove tail meat and roughly chop. Place shells on a foil-lined baking sheet top-side down. Set aside.

3   In a medium skillet over medium heat, add butter and vegetable oil. Once butter is melted and foaming, add onion and cook until soft, about 4 minutes. Add garlic and cook 30 seconds or until fragrant, then add flour and cook 30 seconds.

4   Slowly whisk in brandy or wine, then whisk in half-and-half. Simmer sauce until very thick, about 1 minute. Remove from heat and add tarragon, salt, and pepper, then stir in ¼ cup cheese and chopped lobster meat.

5   Preheat broiler to high.

Continued on next page

6   Stuff shells with lobster mixture. In a small bowl, combine bread crumbs and olive oil, then stir in remaining 2 tablespoons cheese. Top lobster tails with cheesy bread crumbs and broil until bread crumbs are golden brown, about 3 minutes. Garnish with parsley and serve immediately.

Fresh or Frozen?

If you live in a location where it's hard to get your hands on fresh lobster tails, you can opt for frozen ones, which can be found at your local supermarket. You'll just want to thoroughly read the cooking instructions on the package before starting this recipe so you can prepare the lobster tails properly!

HOT AND SOUR SOUP
The Sims 3: Supernatural

Hot and Sour Soup is one of those must-have dishes at a buffet, and for good reason. This dish takes some simple ingredients and, with a little love and a little bit of time, creates a soup worth bragging about. Just don't serve it with a ghost chili like in *The Sims 3*, or you might find yourself breathing fire at the dinner table!

Serves:	Prep Time:	Cook Time:
4	10 minutes	10 minutes

1 cup chicken broth

6 cups water, divided

2 tablespoons soy sauce

1 teaspoon granulated sugar

1 (8-ounce) can bamboo shoots, drained and rinsed

12 ounces fresh shiitake mushrooms, stems removed and sliced

3 tablespoons rice vinegar

¼ teaspoon ground white pepper

1 tablespoon cornstarch

1 large egg, lightly beaten

1 medium green onion, white part removed, chopped

½ teaspoon sesame oil

1. In a medium pot, add broth, $5\frac{3}{4}$ cups water, soy sauce, and sugar. Bring to a boil over medium heat, then stir in bamboo shoots, mushrooms, vinegar, and pepper. Cook around 5 minutes.

2. In a small bowl, combine remaining ¼ cup water and cornstarch. Pour into soup while stirring. Once soup thickens, about 30 seconds, turn off heat and slowly drizzle in beaten egg while gently stirring to form ribbons of egg.

3. Serve hot garnished with onion and oil.

CEVICHE AND CHIPS
The Sims 4: Luxury Party Stuff

Did you spend hours fishing at Desert Bloom Park and come back with just a measly tiny fish? Make the most of that catch and turn it into ceviche, a delicious citrusy fish dish that is paired with chips for scooping.

Serves:	Prep Time:	Cook Time:
4	15 minutes	N/A

1 pound peeled and deveined cooked shrimp, chopped into ¼" pieces

1 cup lime juice

½ medium white onion, peeled and chopped

1 large tomato, seeded and chopped

1 jalapeño pepper, seeded and finely chopped

2 tablespoons finely chopped fresh cilantro

3 tablespoons fresh orange juice

1 tablespoon extra-virgin olive oil

¼ teaspoon salt

1 small avocado, pitted, peeled, and diced

6 cups tortilla chips

1   Add shrimp to a medium glass bowl and add lime juice. Mix well, cover, and refrigerate 30 minutes.

2   In a medium serving bowl, add onion, tomato, jalapeño, and cilantro. Mix well. Drain shrimp and add to serving bowl.

3   In a small bowl, whisk together orange juice, oil, and salt. Pour over shrimp mixture and toss to coat. Add avocado and gently toss to incorporate.

4   Serve immediately with tortilla chips.

Cook Your Own Shrimp
You can find cooked shrimp in the seafood department of most grocery stores, but if you can only find uncooked shrimp, they are easy to cook at home. Thaw and peel 1¼ pounds of shrimp. Bring 2 quarts of water to a boil, then add shrimp. Cook for 1–2 minutes or until opaque and curled into a C shape. Transfer to ice water to stop the cooking.

FISH TACOS
The Sims 4

One of the best street foods out there, Fish Tacos are a really simple meal that packs a lot of flavor. Next time you're at a festival in San Myshuno, be sure to grab yourself some Fish Tacos instead of that pesky Pufferfish Nigiri that might actually kill your Sims. Stay safe out there!

Serves:	Prep Time:	Cook Time:
4	25 minutes	17 minutes

4 (4-ounce) white fish fillets, such as cod or whiting, cut into 2" pieces

1 teaspoon taco seasoning

2 cups finely crushed corn tortilla chips

1 large egg, lightly beaten

3 dashes (¼ plus ⅛ teaspoon) hot sauce

1 tablespoon lime juice

2 teaspoons olive oil

½ teaspoon amber honey

½ teaspoon Dijon mustard

⅛ teaspoon salt

⅛ teaspoon ground black pepper

1½ cups coleslaw mix

8 (6") corn tortillas

½ cup shredded Mexican-style cheese

4 lime wedges

1 Preheat oven to 375°F. Line a baking sheet with aluminum foil lightly greased with nonstick cooking spray.

2 Season fillet pieces with taco seasoning. Set aside.

3 In a shallow dish, add crushed tortilla chips. In a medium dish, add egg and hot sauce and whisk to combine.

4 Dip fish pieces one at a time into egg mixture and allow excess to drip off. Place into tortilla crumbs and roll, patting gently, to coat well. Place on prepared baking sheet with at least ½" between each piece. Repeat until all fish is coated.

5 Bake 12–16 minutes until fish is cooked through, flakes when cut with a fork, and reaches an internal temperature of 145°F.

6 While fish bakes, prepare slaw. In a medium bowl, whisk together lime juice, oil, honey, mustard, salt, and pepper until smooth. Add coleslaw mix and toss to coat. Refrigerate until ready to use.

Continued on next page

7 To assemble, heat tortillas in microwave on high 20 seconds to soften. Divide fish, cheese, and slaw among tortillas. Serve tacos with lime wedges.

DIY Crushed Chips

To get tortilla chip crumbs, just empty a bag of tortilla chips into the food processor and pulse 15–20 times to crush. Once crushed, transfer them to a freezer bag and stash them there for use anytime you need them.

BLACKENED BASS
The Sims 4

If you've spent a long day fishing at Desert Bloom Park, you're bound to come home with a bass. Do you sell it for §20? Or do you turn it into a delicious Blackened Bass for your family to enjoy? Cooking it is the best option, and this recipe is promised to not disappoint any fish lovers who eat it. Pair with a delicious side salad for a perfectly balanced dinner.

Serves:	Prep Time:	Cook Time:
4	20 minutes	20 minutes

2 (1½-pound) whole striped bass, cleaned and scaled

2 tablespoons vegetable oil

3 tablespoons blackening seasoning, such as Zatarain's

4 lemon wedges

1　Rinse fish and pat dry. Make 3–4 diagonal slits to the bone on each side of fish.

2　Brush outsides of fish with oil, then sprinkle both sides with seasoning, rubbing it in to help it adhere.

3　Preheat grill to medium-high and grease a fish grill basket with nonstick cooking spray.

4　Place fish in basket and close to secure. Grill fish 8–10 minutes per side until fish is blackened and a thermometer inserted into thickest part of fish reaches 145°F.

5　Remove fish from basket and let rest 5 minutes before serving. To serve, cut through skin at head and tail of each fish. Slice fish along spine, then use a spoon to slide meat off bones from the back fin and belly. Serve with lemon wedges.

Alternate Cooking Methods
You can also cook this on the stovetop on a grill pan. You will not need the basket, but be sure the grill pan is nonstick.

ROAST CHICKEN
The Sims 4

If you're looking for a great meal to serve at a Dinner Party or on Harvestfest, look no further! Roast Chicken can serve multiple Sims (or humans), and you can add any sides you like to make the meal even more delicious. What makes this recipe even better is that you'll end up with great leftovers for when you don't want to cook tomorrow.

Serves:	Prep Time:	Cook Time:
4	10 minutes	1 hour 5 minutes

1 (4-pound) whole roasting chicken

1 teaspoon sea salt

½ teaspoon ground black pepper

1 large lemon, cut in half

½ medium yellow onion, peeled and cut in half

1   Preheat oven to 450°F and prepare a roasting pan with a rack, or make a ring of foil to keep chicken off bottom of pan.

2   Season outside of chicken with salt and pepper. Insert lemon and onion into breast cavity. Tie chicken legs together with butcher's twine and tuck wings under chicken. Place chicken on roasting rack breast-side up.

3   Roast chicken 25 minutes, then reduce heat to 400°F and roast 30–40 minutes more until a thermometer inserted into thickest part of breast and thigh reaches 165°F.

4   Remove from oven and use tongs to remove lemon and onion from breast cavity. Let rest 10 minutes before carving. Serve alongside lemon and onion.

VEGETABLE DUMPLINGS
The Sims 4

Vegetarian and nonvegetarian Sims alike are lucky to have a recipe like Vegetable Dumplings to add to their weekly meal plan. These dumplings take some of the best vegetables, including mushrooms, carrots, and cabbage, and turn them into something mouthwatering. Just make sure your vegetarian Sims aren't grabbing for meat-filled foods from the fridge: They seem to like to do that sometimes.

Yields:	Prep Time:	Cook Time:
24 dumplings	40 minutes	20 minutes

2 tablespoons vegetable oil, divided

½ medium head napa cabbage, finely shredded (about 3 cups)

1 pint shitake or portobello mushrooms, stems removed and finely chopped

3 medium green onions, chopped

½ medium carrot, finely shredded

1 clove garlic, peeled and finely minced

1 teaspoon grated fresh ginger

1 tablespoon light soy sauce

1 tablespoon hoisin sauce

24 fresh wonton wrappers

1 tablespoon water

¼ teaspoon cornstarch

1 In a large skillet over medium heat, add 1 tablespoon oil. Once hot, add cabbage and cook, stirring often, until wilted, about 3 minutes. Add mushrooms, onion, carrot, garlic, and ginger and cook 1 minute, then add soy sauce and hoisin sauce and stir to combine. Remove from heat and cool 10 minutes.

2 Place 1 tablespoon of filling into center of 1 wonton wrapper. In a small bowl, combine water and cornstarch. Brush one edge of wrapper lightly with water mixture, then fold in half and seal, making sure any excess air is pressed out. Place dumpling on a large plate lightly dusted with cornstarch. Repeat with remaining filling and wrappers. Loosely cover plate with plastic wrap.

3 In a large nonstick skillet over medium heat, add remaining 1 tablespoon oil. Once hot, place dumplings into skillet, leaving ½" between each dumpling. Do not crowd pan; you may need to cook in batches. Cook until dumplings are deeply golden brown on bottom, 3–5 minutes.

4   Add ¼ cup water to pan and cover with a lid. Let steam until liquid has evaporated, about 3 minutes. Transfer dumplings to a large plate and cover with a clean towel while you repeat steaming with any remaining dumplings. Serve hot.

So Many Delicious Options

These dumplings can also be steamed or boiled for soup. To steam, line your steamer with cabbage leaves and cook for 6–8 minutes until dumplings are hot and wrappers are cooked. For boiled dumplings, add to your favorite soup while it's cooking, or simply boil in water or vegetable stock for 6–8 minutes until dumplings are hot and wrappers are tender.

RATATOUILLE
The Sims 3

If you're a huge fan of vegetables, you are absolutely going to love this Ratatouille. The recipe calls for zucchini, bell peppers, onions, and, of course, those giant eggplants you get to grow in *The Sims 4: Cottage Living*. The bigger, the better! Don't worry though: No rats are involved in the creation of this dish.

Serves:	Prep Time:	Cook Time:
4	20 minutes	1 hour 51 minutes

1 (24-ounce) jar tomato purée

½ teaspoon salt

½ teaspoon dry thyme

1 clove garlic, peeled and minced

1 teaspoon granulated sugar

4 teaspoons olive oil, divided

1 medium yellow bell pepper, cored, seeded, and sliced

1 medium red bell pepper, cored, seeded, and sliced

2 large eggplants, trimmed and sliced

2 large zucchini, trimmed and sliced

1 medium white onion, peeled and diced

½ cup fresh grated Parmesan cheese

3 fresh basil leaves, torn into small pieces

1 In a medium pot, add tomato purée, salt, thyme, garlic, and sugar. Stir well, then heat over medium heat until mixture comes to a simmer, about 6 minutes. Reduce heat to low and simmer 40 minutes while you prepare remaining vegetables.

2 In a medium skillet over medium heat, add 1 teaspoon oil. Once hot, add peppers. Sauté until softened, about 10 minutes. Transfer to a medium bowl.

3 To same skillet, add 1 teaspoon oil. Add eggplant and sauté 10 minutes or until eggplant is golden and soft. Transfer to a separate medium bowl.

4 To same skillet, add 1 teaspoon oil. Add zucchini and sauté 5 minutes or until tender. Transfer to a separate medium bowl.

5 To same skillet, add remaining 1 teaspoon oil. Add onions and sauté until tender and just golden around edges, about 10 minutes. Transfer to a separate medium bowl.

6 Strain any accumulated liquid from sautéed vegetables, then add to simmering tomato sauce. Stir well, then increase heat to medium-low and simmer 30 minutes, stirring occasionally.

7 Serve on a large plate garnished with cheese and basil.

CAMPER'S STEW
The Sims 4: Outdoor Retreat

One of the best meals to eat around a campfire, Camper's Stew will keep your belly full and your tent warm all night long. Just make sure you bring an extra bowl to Granite Falls and share with the Hermit: They're pretty lonely out there by themselves.

Serves:	Prep Time:	Cook Time:
4	20 minutes	45 minutes

1 pound ground beef

1 medium white onion, peeled and chopped

1 large russet potato, peeled and diced

1 cup baby carrots (about 12), cut in half

1 clove garlic, peeled and minced

1 (14-ounce) can diced tomatoes, drained

3 cups beef broth

1 (14-ounce) can cut green beans, drained

1 cup frozen whole-kernel corn, thawed

½ teaspoon salt

½ teaspoon ground black pepper

1   In a large Dutch oven or heavy-bottom pot with lid over medium-high heat, add beef. Cook, crumbling beef into chunks, until browned and cooked through, about 10 minutes. Drain off excess fat and return to heat.

2   Add onion and cook until just tender, about 5 minutes, then add potatoes, carrots, garlic, tomatoes, and broth. Stir well, then increase heat to high and bring to a boil. Once boiling, reduce heat to medium-low and simmer 15–20 minutes until potatoes and carrots are tender.

3   Stir in green beans, corn, salt, and pepper. Let simmer 10 minutes until corn and beans are heated through. Serve hot.

MINESTRONE
The Sims 4: Dine Out

There is nothing worse after cooking than having to clean a whole bunch of pots and pans. Luckily, this Minestrone soup only requires one pot! It's not only a delicious recipe; it also won't require you to hire a maid to get your house back in working order.

Serves:	Prep Time:	Cook Time:
6	20 minutes	30 minutes

2 tablespoons olive oil

1 medium yellow onion, peeled and chopped

1 medium carrot, peeled and chopped

1 medium stalk celery, chopped

1 medium zucchini, trimmed and chopped

1 clove garlic, peeled and finely minced

1 (14-ounce) can diced tomatoes, including juice

1 (14-ounce) can kidney beans, drained and rinsed

1 teaspoon Italian seasoning

4 cups chicken stock

1 bay leaf

8 ounces uncooked small pasta, such as tubetti or elbow

½ teaspoon ground black pepper

1 cup fresh-grated Parmesan cheese

1 In a large pot with a lid over medium heat, add oil. Once hot, add onion, carrot, and celery. Cook until just tender, about 5 minutes. Add zucchini and garlic and cook 2 minutes or until zucchini is just starting to get tender around edges.

2 Add tomatoes, beans, Italian seasoning, stock, and bay leaf to pot. Stir well, then increase heat to high and bring to a boil. Once boiling, cover, reduce heat to medium-low, and let simmer 15 minutes.

3 Remove lid and stir well. Remove bay leaf and add pasta. Increase heat to medium and cook until pasta is tender, about 8 minutes.

4 Serve in soup bowls garnished with pepper and cheese.

BUTTER CHICKEN
The Sims 4

A traditional Indian dish, Butter Chicken is a must-try for all foodies out there. This meal is jam-packed with flavor, thanks to the marinade that you coat the chicken with. Your dinner guests will be convinced you just ordered this from Zoomers food delivery.

Serves:	Prep Time:	Cook Time:
4	1 hour 20 minutes	22 minutes

1 pound boneless, skinless chicken breasts, cut into 1" pieces

1 teaspoon garam masala

¼ cup plain Greek yogurt

2 tablespoons salted butter

1 medium white onion, peeled and diced

1 clove garlic, peeled and minced

½ teaspoon ground cumin

1 (12-ounce) jar butter chicken simmer sauce

¼ cup heavy cream

2 cups hot cooked white rice

½ cup frozen peas, thawed

¼ cup chopped fresh parsley

1   In a medium bowl, add chicken and garam masala. Toss to coat chicken in spice, then add yogurt and mix until chicken is coated. Cover and refrigerate 1 hour.

2   In a Dutch oven or deep skillet with a lid over medium heat, add butter. Once melted and foaming, add chicken. Cook until chicken is just cooked through, about 3 minutes per side.

3   Add onion and cook until just tender, about 5 minutes. Add garlic and cumin and cook until fragrant, about 1 minute.

4   Stir in simmer sauce. Let mixture come to a simmer, stirring constantly, and cook 10 minutes. Turn off heat and stir in cream.

5   In a medium bowl, add rice and peas and gently fold to mix.

6   Serve Butter Chicken alongside rice and pea mixture garnished with parsley.

BUTTERNUT GNOCCHI
The Sims 4

If you want to take your gnocchi to the next level and make it absolutely perfect for a Harvest-fest side dish, you'll want to make this recipe. This dish is elegant enough to be served at your next Sim's wedding but simple enough to be a weekday dish for your family. Even Sims with the **foodie** trait will be dying for more.

Serves:	Prep Time:	Cook Time:
4	20 minutes	10 minutes

8 ounces frozen diced butternut squash, thawed

1 tablespoon salt

2 tablespoons salted butter

1 large shallot, peeled and minced

2 cloves garlic, peeled and minced

½ teaspoon sea salt

½ teaspoon ground black pepper

⅓ cup heavy cream

1 (16-ounce) package fresh potato gnocchi

4 fresh sage leaves, chopped

⅓ cup fresh grated Parmesan cheese

1. Place squash in food processor and purée until smooth. Set aside.

2. Fill a large pot with 8 cups water and add salt. Heat over high heat.

3. While water is heating, add butter to a large skillet over medium heat. Once foaming, add shallot and garlic and cook until tender and fragrant, about 1 minute. Add puréed squash, sea salt, and pepper and stir to combine. Once mixture starts to bubble, about 5 minutes, reduce heat to medium-low and stir in cream. Keep warm.

4. Once water is boiling, add gnocchi and cook until gnocchi are floating and hot, 2–3 minutes. Transfer gnocchi with a slotted spoon to skillet with sauce and toss to coat.

5. Serve gnocchi garnished with sage and cheese.

CAESAR SALAD
The Sims 4: Dine Out

Caesar Salad is one of those dishes that you just have to love; the creamy dressing makes it absolutely delicious, and the crunch of the lettuce is something to die for. Making this Caesar Salad at home is easier than building a rocket ship in *The Sims 4*, so get to cooking!

Serves:	Prep Time:	Cook Time:
4	10 minutes	N/A

1 large head romaine lettuce, trimmed and cut into 2" pieces

⅓ cup Caesar salad dressing, such as Cardini's

1 lemon wedge

½ cup shaved Parmesan cheese, divided

1 cup seasoned croutons, divided

1 teaspoon ground black pepper

1   Add lettuce and salad dressing to a large bowl and toss well. Squeeze lemon wedge over salad and toss again.

2   Add ¼ cup cheese and ½ cup croutons and toss, then add remaining ¼ cup cheese and ½ cup croutons to top of salad. Sprinkle pepper over top. Serve immediately.

CHAPTER FOUR
SIDES

Food is important for keeping yourself going, but sometimes regular recipes can get a bit boring. Having side dishes for your go-to meals is an integral part of keeping your time at the dinner table interesting. Side dishes are especially awesome because they can be mixed and matched with so many of your favorite recipes to create a truly unique experience.

In this chapter, you'll find plenty of options when it comes to side dishes, from fun recipes like spooky Cheese Eyeballs and Samosas to more traditional sides like Caprese Salad and Egg Rolls. These are great recipes that can really switch up your plate, and kids can participate, too, since they require a bit less cooking skill and can be made rather quickly. So go ahead and choose your favorite dinner recipe and a perfect side to go along with it: You and your guests are guaranteed to not be disappointed.

BREADSTICKS
The Sims 4: Get to Work

This Breadsticks recipe is a great side for Angry Flaming Spaghetti or as a quick snack in between reading skill books to try to get a promotion. Dip these in your favorite soup on a cool fall day, and you'll be able to conquer the world. Warning: Breadsticks can be extremely addictive and may leave you feeling like a **couch potato**; consume with caution.

Yields:	Prep Time:	Cook Time:
8 breadsticks	2 hours 40 minutes	20 minutes

½ cup whole milk

1 tablespoon granulated sugar

1 teaspoon dry active yeast

1 large egg

4 tablespoons salted butter, melted and cooled

½ teaspoon salt

1 cup all-purpose flour

1 cup bread flour

1 In a small microwave-safe bowl, heat milk on high 20 seconds or until it reaches 110°F. Stir in sugar and yeast and allow to stand until yeast is bubbling and foamy, about 10 minutes.

2 To bowl of a stand mixer fitted with a dough hook or in a large bowl with a wooden spoon, add yeast mixture, egg, and butter. Mix on medium speed until well combined, then add salt and both flours and mix on low 1 minute. Increase speed to medium and knead 4 minutes or until dough is smooth. If mixing by hand, use spoon to stir in flour until dough forms a shaggy ball, then knead in bowl by hand until dough is smooth, about 10 minutes.

3 Form dough into a smooth ball, then cover bowl with a damp towel and let rise in a draft-free spot 1 hour or until doubled in bulk.

4 Preheat oven to 375°F and line a baking sheet with parchment paper.

5   Turn dough out into a lightly floured surface. Press out any air bubbles with your palm. Divide dough into eight pieces and roll each into a 5"-long log. Place each breadstick on prepared sheet. Cover with a damp towel and allow to rise for 30 minutes or until breadsticks are puffy and a finger pressed into side leaves a mark.

6   Bake 18–20 minutes until breadsticks are golden brown on top and bottom. Cool in pan 10 minutes before serving.

Make a Big Batch

These Breadsticks are great because you can easily pop some of them in the freezer to thaw and eat whenever you want them. Cook yourself a big batch, wrap each breadstick individually to avoid freezer burn, and place in a large bag or plastic food container for up to three months. When ready to eat, pop them out of the freezer, let thaw, stick in the oven for a few minutes, and voilà! Fresh, warm breadsticks whenever you want.

ENSAYMADAS
The Sims 4: City Living

There is no better recipe to pair with a bowl of warm soup or to just eat on its own as a nice treat. These Ensaymadas are definitely worth the effort, and the shredded cheese on top really helps to balance the sweetness in the bread. If you've got time on your hands and a desire for cheesy bread in your heart, this is the perfect recipe!

Yields:	Prep Time:	Cook Time:
8 ensaymadas	3 hours 25 minutes	20 minutes

½ cup whole milk

2 tablespoons water

7 tablespoons granulated sugar, divided

1½ teaspoons dry active yeast

2 large egg yolks, at room temperature

6 tablespoons unsalted butter, at room temperature, divided

¼ teaspoon salt

1 cup all-purpose flour

½ cup bread flour

3 tablespoons unsalted butter, melted, divided

½ cup finely shredded mild white Cheddar cheese

1   In a small microwave-safe bowl, combine milk and water. Microwave on high 20 seconds or until mixture reaches 110°F. Stir in 1 tablespoon granulated sugar and yeast and allow to stand until yeast is bubbling and foamy, about 10 minutes.

2   To bowl of a stand mixer fitted with a dough hook or in a large bowl with a wooden spoon, add yeast mixture, 2 tablespoons granulated sugar, egg yolks, and 3 tablespoons butter. Mix on medium speed until combined, then add salt and both flours and mix on low for 1 minute. Increase speed to medium and knead 4 minutes or until dough is smooth. If mixing by hand, use spoon to stir in flour until dough forms a shaggy ball, then knead in bowl by hand until dough is smooth, about 10 minutes. Dough will be very sticky.

3   Scrape dough down from sides of bowl, cover bowl with a damp towel, and let rise in a draft-free spot 2 hours or until doubled in bulk.

4   Grease eight cups of a muffin pan with nonstick cooking spray. Set aside.

Continued on next page

5   Turn dough out onto a well-floured surface. Form dough into a log shape, then cut log into eight equal pieces. Roll each piece into a 4" log, then press each log into an 8" × 4" rectangle. Brush one rectangle with 1 teaspoon melted butter. Roll along long side to form a thin rope. Coil rope into a spiral and place into a prepared muffin cup. Repeat with remaining dough balls. Cover with a damp towel and let rise 1 hour or until double in size.

6   Preheat oven to 350°F.

7   Bake bread 15–20 minutes until golden brown and firm to touch. Remove from pan and transfer to a serving plate. Brush remaining melted butter over the tops and sides.

8   Beat remaining 3 tablespoons butter with 3 tablespoons granulated sugar in a small bowl until smooth. Spread mixture evenly over each roll, then top with cheese while still warm.

9   Sprinkle remaining 1 tablespoon granulated sugar evenly over tops. Allow cheese to melt slightly. Serve.

Motherlode

The most-used cheat in The Sims franchise is **motherlode**. This cheat is used for one specific reason: riches! It will give your Sim's family 50,000 simoleons immediately and can be used over and over again. Absolutely the easiest way to get money in all versions of the game, way easier than your Sims working all day.

EGG ROLLS

The Sims 3: World Adventures and The Sims 4: City Living

The first appearance of Egg Rolls in The Sims was in *The Sims 3: World Adventures*, where you could buy this delicious recipe at the bookstore in Shang Simla. Thankfully, you don't have to travel to a fictional world to eat these delicious Egg Rolls; you can easily make them at home!

Yields:	Prep Time:	Cook Time:
12 egg rolls	30 minutes	30 minutes

½ **pound ground pork**

2 **tablespoons minced white onion**

1 **clove garlic, peeled and minced**

1 **teaspoon fresh grated ginger**

2 **tablespoons hoisin sauce**

1 **tablespoon soy sauce**

½ **teaspoon sesame oil**

4 **cups coleslaw mix**

4 **medium green onions, thinly sliced**

12 **egg roll wrappers**

Vegetable oil, for frying

½ **cup Thai sweet chili sauce**

1   In a medium skillet over medium heat, add pork. Cook, crumbling well, until no longer pink, about 5 minutes. Drain off any fat or liquid and return to heat.

2   Add onion, garlic, and ginger. Cook 1 minute or until garlic and ginger are very fragrant, then add hoisin sauce, soy sauce, and sesame oil. Mix well, then add coleslaw mix and onions. Cook 2–3 minutes until coleslaw is wilted and ingredients are well combined.

3   On a work surface, lay out 1 egg roll wrapper. Place 3 tablespoons of filling into center of wrapper. Fold sides in toward center, then fold edge closest to you over the filling. Wet your finger with water and dampen edge farthest from you. Roll away from you to form an egg roll. Place on a large plate and cover with a towel while you repeat with remaining filling and wrappers.

4   In a large pot with deep sides, add 3" of oil. Heat over medium heat until oil reaches 350°F. Fry 2–3 rolls at a time until they are golden brown on all sides, about 2 minutes per side. Remove from oil and place on a paper towel–lined plate to drain.

5   Serve warm with Thai sweet chili sauce for dipping.

PROSCIUTTO-WRAPPED ASPARAGUS

The Sims 4

If you're looking for a simple side dish that takes very little time and effort to prepare, Prosciutto-Wrapped Asparagus is a great option. This would impress even the **snobbiest** of Sims at your next event. This side dish goes great with meals like Roast Chicken or Blackened Bass.

Serves:	Prep Time:	Cook Time:
4	15 minutes	10 minutes

1 pound asparagus, tough ends trimmed

1 tablespoon olive oil

1 teaspoon fresh lemon zest

¼ teaspoon sea salt

½ pound thin-sliced prosciutto, each slice cut in half lengthwise

¼ teaspoon ground black pepper

2 tablespoons fresh grated Parmesan cheese

1 Preheat oven to 400°F and line a baking sheet with parchment paper.

2 Place asparagus on baking sheet and add oil, lemon zest, and salt. Toss to evenly coat. Wrap each spear with one strip prosciutto and place in a single layer on sheet.

3 Bake 6–10 minutes until prosciutto is browned and asparagus is limp when lifted from tray. Remove from oven and garnish with pepper and cheese. Serve hot.

BUTTERNUT SQUASH SOUP
The Sims 4: Dine Out

There really isn't anything that feels more suited to autumn than a bowl of Butternut Squash Soup. The colors, textures, and taste are just out of this world (like an alien on Planet Sixam). The best thing about this soup is that you can put it next to any protein and it will make a delicious meal.

Serves:	Prep Time:	Cook Time:
6	10 minutes	1 hour 27 minutes

1 (10-ounce) bag fresh or frozen diced butternut squash

1 medium sweet potato, peeled and cubed

1 medium yellow onion, peeled and quartered

2 cloves garlic, peeled

3 tablespoons olive oil

1 teaspoon sea salt

2 tablespoons salted butter

1 medium stalk celery, chopped

1 medium carrot, peeled and chopped

½ teaspoon dry thyme

¼ teaspoon ground cinnamon

¼ teaspoon ground nutmeg

⅛ teaspoon cayenne pepper

4 cups vegetable broth

½ cup plus 2 tablespoons heavy cream, divided

½ teaspoon ground black pepper

6 fresh parsley leaves

1 Preheat oven to 400°F and line a baking sheet with aluminum foil greased with nonstick cooking spray.

2 Add squash, potato, onion, garlic, oil, and salt to sheet. Toss to mix. Roast 45–55 minutes, stirring every 15 minutes, until squash and potatoes are very tender and slightly charred. Remove from oven and set aside to cool while preparing remaining ingredients.

3 In a large Dutch oven or heavy-bottom pot with lid over medium heat, add butter. Once melted, about 30 seconds, add celery and carrot. Sauté until tender, 5–6 minutes. Add thyme, cinnamon, nutmeg, and cayenne pepper and cook until spices are fragrant, about 1 minute.

4 Add roasted vegetables to pot and toss to coat, then add broth. Stir well, then bring to a boil over same heat level, cover with lid, and reduce heat to low. Let soup simmer 20 minutes, then turn off heat and let stand 10 minutes.

5 Working in batches, purée soup in a blender until smooth.

6 Transfer soup back to Dutch oven and place over medium-low heat. Stir in ½ cup cream and heat until warm, 3–5 minutes, making sure not to let soup boil.

7 Drizzle with remaining 2 tablespoons cream and sprinkle with black pepper and parsley leaves. Serve warm.

CHIPS AND SALSA

The Sims 4

Are you looking for the perfect appetizer before a large helping of Blackened Bass? Or a snack between meals? Homemade Chips and Salsa is a great option that is easy to make and tastes fresh and delicious no matter what. This is also the perfect recipe to feed any dinner party guest who may be a glutton before dinner even starts! Looking at you, Eric Lewis.

Serves:	Prep Time:	Cook Time:
8	1 hour 15 minutes	N/A

1 cup prepared tomato salsa

1 Roma tomato, seeded and diced

2 tablespoons chopped fresh cilantro

1 tablespoon minced yellow onion

1 teaspoon fresh lime juice

¼ teaspoon ground cumin

1 (10-ounce) bag tortilla chips

1   In a medium bowl, combine salsa, tomato, cilantro, onion, lime juice, and cumin. Cover and refrigerate at least 1 hour, up to overnight.

2   Serve salsa chilled or at room temperature with tortilla chips.

Easily Improved Chips

Gently warming tortilla chips makes them taste even better with salsa. Spread chips on a baking sheet and place in a 250°F oven for 8–10 minutes or until chips are warm.

CHEESE EYEBALLS

The Sims 4: Spooky Day

Sometimes recipes in The Sims are a little spooky, and this is definitely one of those instances. These Cheese Eyeballs will leave your dinner guests wondering if the eyeballs they're eating are real or truly made of cheese. They are absolutely perfect for your next Spooky Day party! Any finely shredded cheese can be used, so feel free to swap for pepper jack, Mexican blend, Italian blend, smoked Cheddar, Gouda, or any other favorite.

Serves:	Prep Time:	Cook Time:
8	15 minutes	N/A

16 ounces (2 blocks) cream cheese, at room temperature

2 cups finely shredded sharp Cheddar cheese

1 medium green onion, finely chopped

1 tablespoon ranch dressing seasoning mix

⅔ cup finely chopped nuts, such as pecans, almonds, or walnuts

4 pimento-stuffed green olives, sliced in half

1   To bowl of a stand mixer fitted with paddle attachment or in a medium bowl with a hand mixer, add cream cheese. Beat on low speed until creamy and smooth, about 1 minute, then add shredded cheese, onion, and ranch seasoning. Beat until well combined.

2   Line a baking sheet with parchment or wax paper. Scoop mixture onto prepared sheet into eight equal mounds. Cover with plastic wrap and chill 1 hour.

3   Once chilled, remove tray from refrigerator. Lightly oil your hands and form each mound into a ball. Place chopped nuts in a shallow dish and roll each ball into nuts, then place an olive, cut-side facing out, in center of each ball. Serve chilled or at room temperature.

PAN DE MUERTO

The Sims 4

The direct translation of Pan de Muerto is "bread of the dead," so it's probably safe to assume that this is the Grim Reaper's favorite food. This is a traditionally Mexican sweet bread that is served during the few weeks before Dia de los Muertos, or Day of the Dead, a time when people pay their respects to those who have passed in a way that celebrates them. Now you can make it too!

Yields:	Prep Time:	Cook Time:
4 Pan de Muerto	3 hours	22 minutes

½ cup whole milk

4 tablespoons granulated sugar, divided

1 teaspoon dry active yeast

2 large eggs, divided

5 tablespoons unsalted butter, melted and cooled, divided

1 tablespoon plus 1 teaspoon fresh orange zest, divided

½ teaspoon salt

1 cup all-purpose flour

1 cup bread flour

1   In a small microwave-safe bowl, heat milk on high 20 seconds or until it reaches 110°F. Stir in 1 tablespoon sugar and yeast and allow to stand until yeast is bubbling and foamy, about 10 minutes.

2   To bowl of a stand mixer fitted with a dough hook or in a large bowl with a wooden spoon, add yeast mixture, remaining 3 tablespoons sugar, 1 egg, 4 tablespoons butter, and 1 tablespoon orange zest. Mix on medium speed until well combined, then add salt and both flours and mix on low 1 minute. Increase speed to medium and knead 4 minutes or until dough is smooth. If mixing by hand, use spoon to stir in flour until dough forms a shaggy ball, then knead in bowl by hand until dough is smooth, about 10 minutes.

3   Form dough into a smooth ball, then cover bowl with a damp towel and let rise in a draft-free spot 1 hour or until doubled in bulk.

4   Preheat oven to 375°F and line a baking sheet with parchment paper.

5   Turn dough out onto a lightly floured surface. Press out any air bubbles with your palm. Divide dough into five pieces and roll four of them into balls. Divide remaining dough into sixteen pieces, and shape into small bone shapes. Lightly brush dough balls with water. Place two bone shapes on each ball to form a cross shape. Cover with a damp towel and let rise 40 minutes or until double in size.

6   While bread rises, prepare topping. In a small bowl, combine remaining 1 tablespoon sugar and remaining 1 teaspoon orange zest. Rub with your fingers until sugar is very fragrant. Set aside.

7   Beat remaining egg in a small bowl and glaze tops of bread. Place bread on prepared baking sheet and bake 20–22 minutes until loaves are golden brown on top and bottom.

8   Cool on sheet 10 minutes, then brush bread with remaining 1 tablespoon butter and sprinkle over orange sugar topping. Serve warm or at room temperature.

ELOTE

The Sims 4

Elote is a traditional Mexican recipe for grilled corn that makes an excellent side dish for many meals. This recipe first appeared in *The Sims 4* during the Hispanic Heritage Month update and will impress both your Sims and your family members.

Serves:	Prep Time:	Cook Time:
6	15 minutes	7 minutes

1 cup water

6 medium ears corn, husks and silks removed

⅓ cup mayonnaise

¼ cup sour cream

2 teaspoons lime juice

2 tablespoons liquid margarine

½ cup crumbled queso fresco

2 tablespoons finely chopped fresh cilantro

1 teaspoon mild chili powder

6 lime wedges

1   Add water to Dutch oven or large pot with a tight-fitting lid. Place a steamer basket or small heatproof colander into pot. Cover pot and bring to a boil over high heat. Once boiling, carefully remove lid and add corn cobs. Cover and steam 4–7 minutes until corn is tender.

2   While corn cooks combine mayonnaise, sour cream, lime juice, and margarine in a small bowl. Set aside.

3   Carefully remove corn to a large platter. Insert a wooden skewer into bottom of each cob. Brush each cob with mayonnaise mixture, then top with queso, cilantro, and chili powder. Serve immediately with lime wedges for squeezing over corn as you eat.

Don't Break Your Skewer!

Elote ends up being a pretty heavy dish, and you don't want to drop it on the ground or the table while you're trying to eat it. Choose a heavier skewer for the best experience, or use a pair of wood chopsticks as inexpensive wood skewers.

SAMOSAS

The Sims 4: City Living

Next time you're playing the 100 Baby Challenge and looking for a snack that's easy to eat while focused on the screen, try this recipe. Samosas are perfect because you can prepare them in advance and freeze them for up to 3 months, making this a great recipe for when you have many mouths to feed IRL too! For the best results, be sure to thaw these in your fridge overnight before you start to fry them.

Yields:	Prep Time:	Cook Time:
24 Samosas	20 minutes	30 minutes

½ **pound russet potatoes, peeled and cut into ½" cubes**

1 **tablespoon vegetable oil**

¼ **medium white onion, peeled and finely chopped**

¼ **cup frozen green peas**

1 **teaspoon garam masala or curry powder**

½ **teaspoon salt**

¼ **teaspoon ground turmeric**

2 **tablespoons all-purpose flour**

2 **tablespoons water**

6 **(6") flour tortillas, cut into quarters**

Vegetable oil, for frying

1 Place potatoes in a medium pot and add enough water to just cover. Place pot over high heat and bring to a boil. Reduce heat to medium and cook 8–10 minutes until potatoes are fork-tender. Drain well and set aside.

2 In a skillet over medium heat, add oil. Once hot, add onion. Cook until onion is tender, about 3 minutes, then add potatoes, peas, garam masala or curry powder, salt, and turmeric and gently toss to combine. Cook until mixture is hot and spices are well combined, about 1 minute. Set aside to cool 10 minutes.

3 In a small bowl, combine flour and water.

4 Place a tortilla wedge on a work surface with round side facing you. Lightly coat all edges of tortilla with flour paste. Fold left point toward right edge and press to seal, then fold right point toward left edge and press to seal. You should have a point at the top and a point at the bottom formed by the folded tortilla.

5 Pick up tortilla and use your fingers to gently open it like a cone. Fill cone with 1 heaping tablespoon potato mixture. Press opening of cone closed and fold top point over to cover opening and press to seal edges. Add more flour paste if needed to seal well. You should have a triangle-shaped samosa. Repeat with remaining tortillas and filling.

6 Heat 1" of oil in a deep skillet or wide Dutch oven. Once the oil reaches 350°F, add 3–4 samosas and fry 2–3 minutes per side until tortilla is golden brown and crisp. Drain on a paper towel–lined plate. Repeat frying with remaining samosas. Serve hot.

CAPRESE SALAD

The Sims 4

Are you trying to impress your friends with your **gourmet cooking** skill but don't want to go too hard by cooking something like Baked Alaska? A Caprese Salad is a great option! This salad is simple but delicious. It takes very little prep time but is sure to impress every one of your friends.

Serves:	Prep Time:	Cook Time:
4	15 minutes	N/A

2 medium vine-ripened tomatoes, sliced into 8 slices

1 (8-ounce) ball fresh mozzarella, drained and cut into 8 slices

4 fresh basil leaves, thinly sliced

¼ teaspoon sea salt

¼ teaspoon ground black pepper

2 tablespoons extra-virgin olive oil

2 fresh basil leaves

On a serving platter, layer slices of tomato with slices of cheese. Top with sliced basil, salt, and pepper and drizzle oil over top. Place basil leaves in center of salad. Let stand 5 minutes before serving.

Adding Extra Flavor
You can also drizzle 1 tablespoon of balsamic vinegar over this salad if you want to add a touch of sweetness and additional acidity.

DESSERTS

Something that many players have done in The Sims is feed their characters only dessert for days on end—mostly out of laziness since cooking takes too much time. "Oh, you had a birthday? Okay, you're going to eat cake every day for the rest of the week." Of course, this isn't as great of an idea IRL, but the delicious recipes in this chapter are going to have you wishing you *could* eat only dessert.

You'll find classic desserts like Sim-City Cheesecake and Baked Alaska, as well as unique treats like Flirty Heart Cookies and Hamburger Cake, and even a Fruit Cake your guests will love. Thankfully, none of these recipes require you to remodel your home to include a giant cupcake machine, unless that's something you feel compelled to do. Pick your favorites and be sure to bake up these delicious items for your next house party (but don't forget to save yourself some for later).

FLIRTY HEART COOKIES

The Sims 4

Flirty Heart Cookies are created by a Sim who is feeling flirty, and they are really great for setting the mood. These are the kinds of cookies that Don Lothario would have ready for any woman who may enter his home, and they can definitely make sure you're feeling flirty too. Also great for a Love Day party!

Yields:	Prep Time:	Cook Time:
14 cookies	3 hours	24 minutes

1 (17.5-ounce) box sugar cookie mix

¼ cup superfine almond flour

1 teaspoon fresh lemon zest

⅓ cup unsalted butter, at room temperature

1 large egg, at room temperature

½ cup seedless raspberry jam

¼ cup confectioners' sugar

1 Preheat oven to 350°F and line a baking sheet with parchment paper.

2 To bowl of a stand mixer fitted with paddle attachment or in a medium bowl with a hand mixer, add cookie mix, flour, lemon zest, butter, and egg. Mix on medium speed until a stiff dough forms, about 1 minute. Dough will look dry at first, but it will come together and clump around paddle or beaters. Divide dough in half, wrap each half in plastic wrap, and chill 30 minutes.

3 On a lightly floured surface, roll out half of dough to ¼" thickness. With a 2" heart-shaped cookie cutter, cut out fourteen cookies. Place cookies 2" apart on prepared baking sheet.

4 Bake 10–12 minutes until cookies are golden brown around edges. Cool on sheet 10 minutes, then transfer to a cooling rack to cool completely, about 30 minutes.

5 On a lightly floured surface, roll out second half of dough to ¼" thickness. Use the 2" cookie cutter to cut out fourteen hearts. With a smaller heart-shaped cookie cutter or with a sharp paring knife, cut out a small heart from center of each cookie heart.

Continued on next page

6   Place open-heart cookies on prepared baking sheet
    2" apart and bake 10–12 minutes until cookies are
    golden brown around edges. Cool 10 minutes on pan
    before transferring to wire rack to cool completely,
    about 30 minutes.

7   Spread about 1 teaspoon jam on each whole-heart
    cookie. Top with an open-heart cookie. Dust with sugar
    before serving.

FRUIT CAKE
The Sims 4

When the **welcome wagon** comes, do you open the door? Or are you hiding away, trying to act like you don't exist? When you deliver this Fruit Cake, no one will ignore your knock on the door! Feed this to your family, your new neighbors, and your friends.

Yields:	Prep Time:	Cook Time:
24 slices	20 minutes	1 hour 30 minutes

1 (18.25-ounce) box spice cake mix

1 (3.4-ounce) box instant vanilla pudding mix

4 large eggs, at room temperature

½ cup whole milk

½ cup vegetable oil

¼ cup brandy or whiskey

1 teaspoon pure vanilla extract

2 cups chopped mixed candied fruit

½ cup chopped pecans or walnuts

1   Preheat oven to 275°F and grease two 8" × 4" loaf pans with nonstick cooking spray.

2   In a large bowl, combine cake mix and pudding mix. Add eggs, milk, oil, brandy or whiskey, and vanilla. Mix until smooth.

3   Fold in fruit and nuts, then divide mixture evenly between prepared pans. Bake 1 hour 30 minutes or until a toothpick inserted into center of cake comes out clean.

4   Cool cakes completely in pans, about 2 hours. Run a knife or spatula around edges of pan to help cake release before slicing and serving.

Did You Know?
In *The Sims 4*, your Sims are assigned a hidden trait making them either love or hate Fruit Cake. This isn't something you control, but it will determine whether or not your Sims will get a **happy** or **uncomfortable** moodlet when eating it.

AMBROSIA

The Sims 3 and The Sims 4

Ambrosia is an interesting in-game recipe that in *The Sims 4* includes **angel fish**, **death flower**, and a **potion of youth**. Obviously a recipe with a flower, fish, and a magic potion wouldn't taste too great, so this recipe takes a more traditional approach by including some fruit and deliciousness.

Serves:	Prep Time:	Cook Time:
12	3 hours	10 minutes

2 cups graham cracker crumbs

½ cup unsalted butter, melted

⅓ cup granulated sugar

3 cups heavy whipping cream

3 tablespoons instant vanilla pudding mix

⅓ cup confectioners' sugar

2 cups miniature marshmallows

1 (15-ounce) can mandarin oranges, drained and patted dry

1 (15-ounce) can pineapple chunks, drained and patted dry

1 (12-ounce) jar maraschino cherries, drained, patted dry, and sliced in half

1 Preheat oven to 350°F.

2 In a medium bowl, combine graham cracker crumbs, butter, and granulated sugar. Transfer to a 9" × 13" pan and press to create an even base.

3 Bake 10 minutes or until crust is golden and firm. Cool completely, about 30 minutes.

4 To bowl of a stand mixer fitted with whip attachment or in a large bowl with a hand mixer, add cream, pudding mix, and confectioners' sugar. Mix on low speed until sugar and pudding mix are incorporated, then increase speed to high and whip until soft peaks form, 2–3 minutes. Fold in marshmallows with a spatula, then spread mixture on prepared graham crust.

5 Decorate top with oranges, pineapples, and cherries. Chill 2 hours before serving.

Fun Fact

Did you know that in both *The Sims 3* and *The Sims 4*, having a ghost consume a single serving of Ambrosia will bring them back to life? This is hands-down one of the most powerful recipes to make in the game, requiring your Sims to get their hands on some expensive and hard-to-find ingredients.

SIMCITY CHEESECAKE
The Sims 4

This delicious cheesecake was named after the great city builder, SimCity, a huge inspiration for The Sims. It's delicious and can be made even better with slight adjustments (i.e., toppings), just like any city you made in SimCity 3000. Just be sure to not build a house on top of the cheesecake: That wouldn't go well.

Serves:	Prep Time:	Cook Time:
12	8 hours	1 hour 20 minutes

1½ cups graham cracker crumbs

⅓ cup unsalted butter, melted

1¼ cups granulated sugar, divided

2 cups hot water

4 (8-ounce) blocks cream cheese, at room temperature

1 tablespoon cornstarch

4 large eggs, at room temperature

1 cup sour cream

¼ cup heavy cream

1 teaspoon pure vanilla extract

1 Preheat oven to 350°F.

2 In a medium bowl, combine graham cracker crumbs, butter, and ¼ cup sugar. Transfer to a 9" springform pan and press to create an even base.

3 Bake 10 minutes or until crust is golden and firm. Cool completely, about 30 minutes.

4 In a large ovenproof dish, add water. Place dish on bottom rack of oven.

5 In a large bowl, add cream cheese. Use a hand mixer to beat on medium speed until smooth and no lumps remain. Add remaining 1 cup sugar and cornstarch and mix well, then add eggs one at a time and mix until completely incorporated. Reduce speed to low and add sour cream, heavy cream, and vanilla. Mix until well blended and no streaks of white remain.

6 Pour batter over crust in springform pan. Use a spatula to smooth out batter, then tap pan on counter 3–4 times to release any air bubbles.

7   Bake cheesecake 20 minutes, then reduce heat to
    325°F and bake 40–50 minutes until cheesecake is set
    around edges but still slightly jiggly in center.

8   Turn off heat and let cheesecake stand in oven 1 hour,
    then crack oven door and let stand 1 hour more before
    removing. Cool in pan on counter 1 hour, then cover
    with plastic wrap and chill 4 hours or overnight.

9   Run a knife or spatula around edges of pan before
    removing ring. Serve chilled.

HAMBURGER CAKE
The Sims 4

When you hear the words "Hamburger Cake," you may wonder, "Why would one want to eat a cake made of beef?" Well, no need to worry: This cake just *looks* like a hamburger! This recipe comes with *The Sims 4: Deluxe Edition*, and has been a favorite of players for years.

Serves:	Prep Time:	Cook Time:
14	4 hours	45 minutes

2 (18.25-ounce) boxes chocolate cake mix

8 large eggs

2 cups buttermilk

1 cup unsalted butter, melted and cooled

Brown gel food coloring

1 (16-ounce) can vanilla frosting

1 (16-ounce) can chocolate frosting

8 ounces green fondant

8 ounces yellow fondant

1 ounce orange fondant

¼ cup crispy rice cereal

1   Preheat oven to 350°F and grease two 8" cake pans and one 2½-quart ovenproof bowl with nonstick cooking spray.

2   In a large bowl, add cake mix, eggs, buttermilk, and butter. Mix until smooth, with only a few small lumps remaining.

3   Divide batter equally between prepared pans and bowl. Bake pans 25–30 minutes, and bake bowl 40–45 minutes until cakes spring back when pressed in center and start to come away from sides of pans. Cool in pans and bowl 10 minutes before turning out onto a wire rack to cool to room temperature, about 2 hours.

4   In a small bowl, add food coloring to vanilla frosting 1 drop at a time while mixing until frosting resembles the color of a hamburger bun.

5   Trim cake layers baked in pans, if needed, to flatten if domed. Trim bottom of cake baked in bowl, if needed, so bottom is flat.

6   Place one 8" cake on a serving platter and frost with ⅓ vanilla frosting on top and sides.

Continued on next page

7 Place second 8" cake layer on a separate plate and frost with chocolate frosting on top and sides. Carefully place on top of first cake.

8 Roll out green fondant and cut a 4" circle. Ruffle edges to resemble lettuce. Place on chocolate frosted cake.

9 Combine yellow and orange fondant until color is even, then roll out. Cut out a 4" square. Lay square over green fondant "lettuce."

10 Place bowl-shaped cake on top of yellow fondant square and frost on top and sides with remaining vanilla frosting. Sprinkle with rice cereal. Serve.

BAKED ANGEL FOOD CAKE
The Sims 3

If you're looking for a lighter cake recipe for your next event, a Baked Angel Food Cake is the solution to all your problems. This cake is best topped with a bit of whipped cream or frosting and some fresh fruit, especially strawberries. Perfect for your next dinner party dessert.

Serves:	Prep Time:	Cook Time:
10	2 hours 45 minutes	45 minutes

1 (16-ounce) box angel food cake mix

1⅓ cups water

1 (8-ounce) block cream cheese, at room temperature

½ cup unsalted butter, at room temperature

1 teaspoon pure vanilla extract

3 cups confectioners' sugar, divided

1½ cups strawberry jam, divided

½ cup fruit cocktail, drained well

1 Preheat oven to 350°F and line bottom of a glass or metal 9" × 13" pan with parchment paper.

2 In a large glass or metal bowl, add cake mix and water. With a hand mixer, beat on low speed until cake mix is just moistened, about 30 seconds, then increase speed to medium and beat until fluffy, about 1 minute. Transfer batter to prepared pan and smooth to make an even layer.

3 Bake 35–45 minutes until cake is dry and crusty on top and a toothpick inserted into center of cake is clean.

4 Place a wire rack on top of cake pan, carefully flip over, and allow cake to cool upside down 2 hours.

5 While cake cools, prepare frosting. To bowl of a stand mixer fitted with paddle attachment or in a medium bowl with a hand mixer, add cream cheese and butter. Beat on medium speed until well combined and creamy, about 1 minute. Add vanilla and 1 cup sugar and beat on low to combine, about 30 seconds. Add remaining sugar 1 cup at a time, beating 30 seconds on low after each addition. Once smooth, cover with plastic wrap until ready to use.

Continued on next page

6 To assemble, turn cake pan over and run a knife or metal spatula around edges of pan to release cake. Place a cutting board over top of pan and flip over. Lift pan and peel back parchment.

7 Facing long side of cake, cut ⅓ of cake off one side and reserve. Place bottom cake on serving platter. With a serrated knife, cut larger cake in half horizontally. Spread 1 cup jam on bottom of larger cake. Replace top of cake and frost top with cream cheese frosting.

8 With a serrated knife, cut smaller cake in half horizontally. Place bottom of smaller cake on top of larger cake and spread remaining ½ cup jam on top. Replace top of cake and spread with cream cheese frosting, letting some frosting drip down sides of cakes. Chill 30 minutes. Spoon fruit cocktail into center of cake just before serving.

GRILLED FRUIT
The Sims 4

If you're looking for a nice dessert that's supersweet but also healthy, Grilled Fruit is perfect. This dessert can be cooked on a barbecue or grill top and is perfect for satisfying that sweet tooth. You can even add spices like cinnamon or nutmeg for a more interesting flavor profile, or keep it simple and just enjoy the warm fruit.

Serves:	Prep Time:	Cook Time:
4	35 minutes	4 minutes

1 medium peach, pitted and cut into 8 slices

2 medium-sized firm bananas, cut into 4 pieces each

1 cup (about 8 pieces) fresh pineapple chunks

8 fresh strawberries, hulled and stems removed

2 tablespoons amber honey

1 Soak four long wood skewers in water for 20 minutes.

2 Preheat grill or grill pan to medium and grease grates lightly with nonstick cooking spray.

3 Thread fruit onto skewers alternating between peach slices, banana pieces, pineapple chunks, and strawberries.

4 Grill skewers 1–2 minutes per side until fruit is hot and slightly charred. Transfer to serving platter and drizzle with honey. Serve immediately.

BAKED ALASKA
The Sims 2 and *The Sims 4*

This was possibly one of the most dangerous meals to make in *The Sims 2* because your Sims would often set their house on fire trying to flambé the dish. Luckily, this recipe was created with safety in mind. It has all the components of an awesome dessert, with pound cake, vanilla ice cream, and sugar.

Serves:	Prep Time:	Cook Time:
4	2 hours 30 minutes	3 minutes

4 (1") slices pound cake

1 quart vanilla ice cream

4 egg whites

¼ teaspoon cream of tartar

¼ cup granulated sugar

1 With a round biscuit cutter, cut each slice of pound cake into a circle. Discard scraps.

2 Scoop ice cream onto each cake round. Transfer to freezer for 2 hours.

3 Preheat broiler to high and place rack in top third of oven. Line a baking sheet with parchment paper.

4 In a medium metal bowl with a hand mixer, add egg whites and cream of tartar. Beat on medium speed until egg whites are frothy, about 1 minute. Increase speed to medium-high and beat, adding sugar 1 tablespoon at a time, until egg whites are stiff and glossy, about 2 minutes.

5 Remove cakes from freezer and transfer to prepared baking sheet. Quickly spread meringue over all sides of ice cream and cake rounds.

6 Broil 2–3 minutes until meringue is browned. Serve immediately.

How to Avoid Melting
The meringue will help hold in any ice cream that starts to melt while in the oven, so be sure to completely cover the ice cream and pound cake all the way to the bottom.

MINTY MOCHA CUPCAKES
The Sims 4

Is there any better flavor pairing than mint and chocolate? Doubtful. You'll be wanting to share these delicious cupcakes with all your friends, especially around the holidays. Leaving one of these out for Father Winter will guarantee that he gives you a large gift and not a lump of coal.

Yields:	Prep Time:	Cook Time:
12 cupcakes	1 hour 25 minutes	20 minutes

1 tablespoon instant espresso powder

3 tablespoons hot water

¾ cup all-purpose flour

⅓ cup cocoa powder

¾ cup granulated sugar

1 teaspoon baking powder

¼ teaspoon baking soda

¼ teaspoon salt

⅓ cup buttermilk

4 tablespoons unsalted butter, melted and cooled

1 large egg

1 large egg white

1 teaspoon pure vanilla extract

½ cup unsalted butter, at room temperature

3 cups confectioners' sugar

¼ cup whole milk

¼ teaspoon mint extract

3 drops green gel food coloring

½ cup chocolate syrup

12 chocolate-covered espresso beans

1. Preheat oven to 350°F and line a twelve-cup cupcake pan with paper liners.

2. In a small bowl add espresso powder and whisk in hot water. Set aside to cool, about 10 minutes.

3. In a medium bowl, combine flour, cocoa powder, granulated sugar, baking powder, baking soda, and salt. Set aside.

4. In a large bowl, add prepared espresso, buttermilk, melted butter, egg, egg white, and vanilla. Whisk until well combined, then pour into dry ingredients and mix until smooth, with only a few small lumps remaining.

5. Divide batter evenly into prepared cupcake pan and bake 18–20 minutes until cupcakes spring back when gently pressed in center and a toothpick inserted in center comes out clean. Cool 5 minutes in pan, then transfer cupcakes to a wire rack to cool completely, about 1 hour.

6   While cupcakes cool, prepare frosting. To bowl of a stand mixer fitted with paddle attachment or in a medium bowl with a hand mixer, add room temperature butter. Mix on low speed until creamy, then add confectioners' sugar, milk, mint extract, and food coloring. Beat on low 30 seconds, then increase speed to medium and beat until smooth and fluffy, about 2 minutes. If you would like a deeper green color, add 1–2 more drops of food coloring.

7   To assemble, frost tops of cupcakes with mint frosting. Drizzle each with chocolate syrup, then place an espresso bean on top of each cupcake.

PLUMBOB SUGAR COOKIES

The Sims 4: Get to Work

Sugar cookies are one of the most creative desserts because you can really make them into any shape. Of course, for this recipe they *had* to be made into Plumbobs! These diamond-shaped sugar cookies can be decorated in any color to match your mood, and you can hold one above your head for a cute photo moment that'll make you feel like a Sim IRL.

Yields:	Prep Time:	Cook Time:
4 dozen cookies	2 hours 45 minutes	12 minutes

1 cup salted butter, at room temperature

1 cup granulated sugar

1 large egg, at room temperature

1 teaspoon pure vanilla extract

3 cups all-purpose flour

1 teaspoon baking soda

¼ teaspoon salt

¼ cup whole milk

½ cup green sugar sprinkles

1 To bowl of a stand mixer fitted with paddle attachment or in a large bowl with a hand mixer, add butter and sugar. Mix on medium speed until mixture is creamy and fluffy, about 3 minutes. Add egg and vanilla and mix on low until egg is fully incorporated, about 1 minute.

2 In a separate large bowl, sift together flour, baking soda, and salt. Add to butter mixture alternately with milk in three additions, mixing on low until just combined, about 15 seconds per addition. Once everything is combined, increase speed to medium and mix until no dry flour remains and mixture is uniform, about 30 seconds. Wrap dough in plastic wrap, form into a flat disk, and chill 1 hour.

3 Preheat oven to 375°F and line two baking sheets with parchment paper.

4 Divide dough in half, leaving one half in refrigerator. Place other half of dough on lightly floured surface and roll into a ¼" circle. Using a diamond-shaped cutter, cut into twenty-four cookies. Transfer cookies to prepared baking sheets, leaving 2" between each cookie. Sprinkle cookies with sugar sprinkles.

Continued on next page

Repeat with remaining chilled dough. Cookies that do not fit on baking sheets should be placed on a plate and chilled until ready to make. Any leftover dough should be formed into a disk, wrapped in plastic, and chilled for 30 minutes before rerolling.

5 Bake cookies 9–12 minutes until just golden brown around edges and firm in center. Cool 10 minutes on pan before transferring to a wire rack to cool completely, about 30 minutes.

Finding the Perfect Cutters
Plumbob-shaped cookie cutters are available online. Look for cutters with sharp corners for the best result. If the cutters are not available, you can use a sharp paring knife and a template cut from paper.

BAKED CHOCOLATE MOUSSE

The Sims 4

If you're ever feeling like you need to exercise your **glutton** trait but don't want to feel too weighed down, a Baked Chocolate Mousse is the best! This dessert is rich and decadent, but the egg whites allow it to be light and airy; it will not disappoint. Plus, this recipe makes a single serving so you can make it just for you, no sharing necessary!

Serves:	Prep Time:	Cook Time:
1	1 hour	36 minutes

1½ tablespoons salted butter, at room temperature

2 ounces finely chopped bittersweet chocolate

1 large egg, yolk and white separated

¹⁄₁₆ teaspoon cream of tartar

2 tablespoons granulated sugar, divided

¼ teaspoon pure vanilla extract

2 tablespoons whipped cream

1 Preheat oven to 350°F.

2 In a small microwave-safe bowl, add butter and chocolate. Microwave on high 30 seconds, stir well, then microwave in 15-second intervals until fully melted. Set aside.

3 In a medium bowl, add egg white and cream of tartar. Use a hand mixer to beat on medium speed until foamy, about 30 seconds, then gradually add 1 tablespoon sugar and beat on high until stiff peaks form, about 1 minute. Set aside.

4 In a small bowl with a hand mixer, beat together egg yolk, vanilla, and remaining 1 tablespoon sugar until light in color, about 2 minutes. Add chocolate mixture to egg yolk mixture and mix to combine, about 20 seconds.

5 Fold half of egg white into chocolate mixture until just combined, then add remaining egg white and fold in until no streaks remain.

6 Spoon batter into an ungreased 8-ounce ramekin. Bake 30–35 minutes until puffed yet still jiggly in center. Transfer to a wire rack to cool completely to room temperature, about 40 minutes. Top with whipped cream before serving.

KEY LIME PIE
The Sims 3

There is nothing more comforting than a refreshing slice of Key Lime Pie; it's maybe even better than a bowl of Grandma's Comfort Soup. Those little fruits are good for more than just making your drinks more delicious: The lime flavor is sure to knock your socks off. Just make sure you pick them up off the floor, or the monster under the bed might eat them before he scares the next kid.

Serves:	Prep Time:	Cook Time:
8	5 hours 30 minutes	25 minutes

1¼ cups graham cracker crumbs

6 tablespoons unsalted butter, melted and cooled

2 tablespoons granulated sugar

1 (14-ounce) can sweetened condensed milk

4 large egg yolks

⅔ cup key lime juice

2 tablespoons whipped topping

5 thin lime wedges

1 Preheat oven to 350°F.

2 In a medium bowl, combine graham cracker crumbs, butter, and sugar. Transfer to a 9" pie pan and press evenly into bottom and sides. Bake 10 minutes or until crust is golden and firm. Cool completely, about 30 minutes.

3 In a separate medium bowl, add condensed milk, egg yolks, and lime juice. Whisk until smooth and starts to thicken, about 1 minute.

4 Pour filling into prepared crust. Bake 10–15 minutes or until filling is set around edges and slightly wobbly in center. Remove from oven and cool to room temperature, about 1 hour, before covering and refrigerating 4 hours up to overnight.

5 To garnish, spoon whipped topping into center of pie. Arrange lime wedges in a circle around whipped topping. Serve chilled.

ALMOND MACARONS
The Sims 4: Luxury Party Stuff

Almond Macarons are one of the more complicated dessert recipes in The Sims. Even Sims with a level 10 **baking** skill would struggle their first few times, but the delicious result is always worth the effort. This recipe gives easy-to-follow steps and tips to help you get the perfect-quality macaron in no time!

Yields:	Prep Time:	Cook Time:
20 macarons	3 hours 30 minutes	18 minutes

1 teaspoon lemon juice

3 very fresh large egg whites

¼ teaspoon cream of tartar

¼ teaspoon pure vanilla extract

¼ teaspoon almond extract

⅓ cup superfine sugar

1¼ cups superfine almond flour

1¼ cups confectioners' sugar

1 cup chocolate frosting, divided

20 whole roasted unsalted almonds

1   To a medium metal bowl, add lemon juice. Use a paper towel to wipe all surfaces of bowl with lemon juice. Allow bowl to dry, then add egg whites and let stand until they reach room temperature, about 30 minutes.

2   To egg whites, add cream of tartar, vanilla, and almond extract. With a hand mixer, beat egg whites on medium speed until very frothy, about 1 minute. Add superfine sugar 1 tablespoon at a time while continuing to beat egg whites. Once all sugar is added, increase speed to high and beat until egg whites form glossy, stiff peaks that do not droop. Set aside.

3   In a food processor, add almond flour and confectioners' sugar. Pulse 10–15 times to thoroughly combine and break up any lumps. Sift mixture into a medium bowl, discarding any larger pieces of almond. Do not discard more than 1 tablespoon.

4   Fold egg whites into almond flour mixture in three additions by drawing a spatula down through middle of mixture and folding up over top, rotating bowl ¼ turn and repeating. This whole process should take about

50 strokes. Your batter is ready when a small amount dropped off a spatula takes about 10 seconds to sink back into the batter. If batter is too thick, you can continue to fold until the right consistency is achieved. Do not overmix.

5   Line two baking sheets with parchment paper.

6   Load batter into a piping bag fitted with a large round tip (such as Wilton 1A). Holding bag directly over parchment at a 90° angle, pipe forty 1" mounds onto sheet about 1" apart. Rap sheet pans on counter three times to release any air bubbles. If any appear on tops of cookies, use a toothpick to pop them.

7   Let piped cookies stand at room temperature 30–45 minutes until tops are no longer sticky.

8   Preheat oven to 325°F.

9   Bake 15–18 minutes until cookies are firm and shiny and there is a ⅛" "foot" around bottom of cookies. Cool completely on baking sheets to room temperature, about 30 minutes.

10 Spread 1–2 teaspoons of frosting on twenty of the cookies and top with remaining cookies to make sandwiches. Dip one side of almonds into frosting and place them on top of cookies. Enjoy immediately or refrigerate in a covered container up to 5 days.

Tips for Perfecting

The absolute key to making a delicious macaron is the consistency of your batter. You can always tell how well this dessert will turn out before you ever even bake them. Your batter should have a thick consistency (if you lift a spoonful of the mixture and drizzle it back in a firm line or ribbon, it will disappear into the remaining mixture in about 10 seconds). You got this!

STRAWBERRY FIZZY CUPCAKES
The Sims 4

These adorably pink cupcakes are great for surprising your guests with new sensations: They are filled with popping candy that explodes on your taste buds. They are almost as explosive as some detonation packs your Sims could explode in *The Sims 3: Ambitions*; just make sure to not let these cupcakes explode IRL.

Yields:	Prep Time:	Cook Time:
12 cupcakes	1 hour 20 minutes	20 minutes

1 cup all-purpose flour

¾ cup granulated sugar

1 teaspoon baking powder

¼ teaspoon baking soda

¼ teaspoon salt

¼ cup buttermilk

½ cup strawberry jam, divided

4 tablespoons vegetable oil

1 large egg

1 large egg white

1 teaspoon pure vanilla extract

6–10 drops red gel food coloring, divided

½ cup unsalted butter, at room temperature

3 cups confectioners' sugar

1 tablespoon whole milk

½ cup strawberry popping candy

6 fresh strawberries, sliced in half

1 Preheat oven to 350°F and line a twelve-cup cupcake pan with paper liners.

2 In a medium bowl, combine flour, granulated sugar, baking powder, baking soda, and salt. Set aside.

3 In a large bowl, add buttermilk, ¼ cup jam, oil, egg, egg white, and vanilla. Whisk until well combined, then pour into dry ingredients along with 3 drops food coloring and mix until smooth, with only a few small lumps remaining. If you want a deeper pink color, add 1–2 more drops of food coloring.

4 Divide batter evenly into prepared cupcake pan and bake 18–20 minutes until cupcakes spring back when gently pressed in center and a toothpick inserted in center comes out clean. Cool 5 minutes in pan, then transfer cupcakes to a wire rack to cool completely, about 1 hour.

Continued on next page

5   While cupcakes cool, prepare frosting. To bowl of a stand mixer fitted with paddle attachment or in a medium bowl with a hand mixer, add butter. Mix on low speed until creamy, then add confectioners' sugar, remaining ¼ cup jam, milk, and remaining 3 drops food coloring. Beat on low 30 seconds, then increase speed to medium and beat until smooth and fluffy, about 2 minutes. If you would like a deeper pink color, add 1–2 more drops food coloring.

6   To assemble, swirl frosting on tops of cupcakes and sprinkle with popping candy. Garnish each cupcake with a strawberry half, cut-side down.

TIRAMISU
The Sims 4: Dine Out

Are you in for a long night of studying at the Foxbury Institute and really need a pick-me-up? Well, why not eat a delicious dessert that will also give you a bit of a caffeine hit from espresso?! You'll find yourself and your Sims finishing the entire semester's worth of homework in one night after consuming even half of this Tiramisu.

Serves:	Prep Time:	Cook Time:
8	3 hours 25 minutes	N/A

2 cups heavy whipping cream

½ cup confectioners' sugar

1 teaspoon pure vanilla extract

1 (8-ounce) package mascarpone cheese, at room temperature

2 (7-ounce) packages ladyfingers

2 cups cold espresso

2 tablespoons cocoa powder

1. In a large bowl, add cream, sugar, and vanilla. With a hand mixer, beat on low speed until ingredients are combined, about 30 seconds, then increase speed to high and whip until soft peaks form. Transfer ½ cup to a separate bowl and refrigerate.

2. To whipped cream, add mascarpone and fold to combine. Cover and refrigerate 1 hour.

3. Line a 9" springform pan with a strip of parchment paper around side of pan.

4. Dip ladyfingers into espresso 1–2 seconds until just soaked, then place on bottom of pan. You may need to break some into smaller pieces to cover bottom. Remove mascarpone mixture from fridge and smooth half of mixture over tops of ladyfingers. Dip remaining ladyfingers into espresso and cover mascarpone layer. Top with remaining mascarpone mixture, smoothing top with a spatula.

5. Cover and refrigerate 2 hours. Once chilled, carefully open springform and remove parchment strip. Dust top with cocoa powder. Use a piping bag to decorate top with remaining ½ cup whipped cream. Enjoy chilled.

CHOCOLATE CAKE
The Sims 4

It's time to **age up**! Chocolate Cake is a must-have at any good birthday celebration in The Sims, and this recipe is perfect for any IRL celebration. Decorated with rainbow sprinkles, this cake will be a family-requested treat.

Serves:	Prep Time:	Cook Time:
12	2 hours 40 minutes	35 minutes

1½ cups all-purpose flour

⅔ cups cocoa powder plus ¼ cup, divided

1 teaspoon baking powder

½ teaspoon baking soda

½ teaspoon salt

1½ cups granulated sugar

½ cup vegetable oil

1 cup buttermilk, at room temperature

4 large eggs, at room temperature

1½ teaspoons pure vanilla extract, divided

¾ cup unsalted butter, at room temperature

4 cups confectioners' sugar

¼ cup whole milk

2 tablespoons rainbow sprinkles

1 Preheat oven to 350°F and grease two 8" cake pans with nonstick cooking spray and line bottoms with circles of parchment paper.

2 In a large bowl, add flour, ⅔ cup cocoa powder, baking powder, baking soda, and salt. Whisk to combine. Set aside.

3 In a medium bowl, add granulated sugar, oil, buttermilk, eggs, and 1 teaspoon vanilla. Whisk to combine, then add to flour mixture and mix until batter is smooth, with a few small lumps remaining.

4 Divide batter between prepared pans. Bake 30–35 minutes until cake springs back when gently pressed in center and starts to come away from sides of pan. Cool in pans 10 minutes, then turn out onto wire racks, remove parchment, and cool to room temperature, about 2 hours.

5 While cakes cool, prepare frosting. In a medium bowl, add butter and remaining ¼ cup cocoa powder. With a hand mixer, beat on low speed until ingredients are incorporated and mixture is creamy, about 1 minute.

Add confectioners' sugar, milk, and remaining ½ teaspoon vanilla and beat on low until ingredients are incorporated, about 1 minute. Increase speed to medium and beat 1–2 minutes until frosting is creamy and fluffy.

6 Once cakes are cooled, place one layer on a serving plate. Spread half of frosting on top of cake to edges, then place second cake layer on top, bottom-side down. Frost top and sides of cake and decorate top with sprinkles.

ALIEN FRUIT TARTS
The Sims 4: Get to Work

Did you recently take a trip to Sixam? Are you trying to impress the new alien friends you just made? Well, some Alien Fruit Tarts are your best option to keep those aliens in your life forever. These fruit tarts are delicious and are definitely not a mysterious color...not at all. Best served with a fresh cup of tea or coffee—if the aliens will drink it.

Serves:	Prep Time:	Cook Time:
6	2 hours 15 minutes	N/A

1 (5.1-ounce) box instant vanilla pudding mix

3 cups whole milk

3 drops green gel food coloring

2 drops blue gel food coloring

6 prepared (20 grams each) mini graham cracker piecrusts

½ cup fresh blueberries

1 medium kiwi, peeled and sliced

1 In a medium bowl, add pudding mix, milk, and green and blue food coloring. Whisk until mixture is smooth and color is even. Cover and chill 2 hours.

2 Once chilled, divide pudding between graham cracker crusts. Arrange blueberries and kiwi on top. Serve chilled.

Slight Variation

In *The Sims 4*, the Alien Fruit Tarts are made with the UFO (Unidentified Fruit Object). Since you don't have access to real-life alien fruit, this recipe uses some fruit you'll find right here on earth. Hopefully someday you can take a trip to Sixam and grab some UFO for yourself.

APPLE PIE

The Sims 4

Apple Pie is one of those desserts that you know your Sims will be eating at Harvestfest right after they get into a fight with a gnome that just wouldn't play along. Why do they leave seeds everywhere anyway? Well, now you can make an Apple Pie for your IRL celebrations to impress all your family members and friends!

Serves:	Prep Time:	Cook Time:
8	3 hours 30 minutes	55 minutes

1 (14.1-ounce) box prepared refrigerated piecrusts

½ cup packed light brown sugar

4 cups thinly sliced Granny Smith or Pink Lady apples

2 tablespoons unsalted butter

1 teaspoon ground cinnamon

3 tablespoons cornstarch

3 tablespoons water

2 teaspoons pure vanilla extract

2 tablespoons whole milk

2 tablespoons granulated sugar

1 Remove one piecrust from package and unroll on a lightly floured work surface. Lay crust into a 9" pie plate and lift edges to help crust slide down sides of pan. Cover with plastic wrap and refrigerate while making pie filling.

2 In a medium saucepan, add brown sugar, apples, butter, and cinnamon. Cook over medium heat until apple mixture comes to a boil and apples are tender, about 5 minutes.

3 In a small bowl, combine cornstarch and water. Pour over apple mixture and stir well to combine. Once mixture thickens, about 30 seconds, turn off heat and add vanilla. Set aside to cool 20 minutes.

4 Preheat oven to 400°F and place a baking sheet on rack in bottom third of oven.

5 Remove second piecrust and unroll on a lightly floured surface. Cut into eight 1" strips.

6   Remove first crust from refrigerator and uncover. Spoon apple filling into crust. Arrange piecrust strips over filling in a lattice pattern. Trim edge of crust to $\frac{1}{2}$" and tuck under. Flute with fingers or crimp with a fork. Brush with milk and sprinkle with granulated sugar.

7   Place pie on baking tray in the oven. Bake 10 minutes, then reduce heat to 350°F and bake 35–40 minutes until filling is bubbling and crust is golden brown. Cool completely to room temperature, about 3 hours, before serving.

BLACK AND WHITE COOKIES
The Sims 4

Are you looking to throw a classy Black and White party for your next event? Well, a batch of Black and White Cookies will work perfectly. Even Nancy Landgraab will be impressed by the fact that the cookies followed the dress code, but will she follow it herself? Probably not; she's always gotta be the center of attention!

Yields:	Prep Time:	Cook Time:
12 cookies	2 hours 15 minutes	18 minutes

½ cup unsalted butter, at room temperature

1 cup granulated sugar

⅓ cup sour cream

1 large egg

½ teaspoon pure vanilla extract

½ teaspoon fresh lemon zest

2 cups all-purpose flour

1 tablespoon cornstarch

¾ teaspoon baking soda

¾ teaspoon baking powder

5 cups confectioners' sugar

6 tablespoons whole milk, divided

1 teaspoon clear vanilla extract

3 tablespoons Dutch process cocoa powder

1   Preheat oven to 350°F and line two baking sheets with parchment paper.

2   To bowl of a stand mixer fitted with paddle attachment or in a large bowl with a hand mixer, add butter and granulated sugar. Beat on medium speed until smooth and fluffy, about 1 minute. Add sour cream, egg, pure vanilla, and lemon zest and beat until well combined, about 1 minute.

3   In a medium bowl, add flour, cornstarch, baking soda, and baking powder. Whisk to combine. Add flour mixture to butter mixture and mix on low speed 30 seconds, then increase speed to medium and beat until a smooth dough forms, 30–40 seconds.

4   Use a ¼-cup measuring cup to scoop dough onto prepared baking sheets at least 4" apart. You should have six cookies per sheet. Bake 15–18 minutes until cookies are golden brown and firm in center. Cool on baking sheets to room temperature, about 30 minutes. If baking both pans at the same time, be sure to rotate pans after 8 minutes to ensure even baking.

5   While cookies cool, prepare icings. In a medium bowl, add confectioners' sugar, 5 tablespoons milk, and clear vanilla. Whisk until smooth. Measure 1 cup of icing and transfer to a smaller bowl. Add remaining 1 tablespoon milk and cocoa powder to smaller bowl and whisk until smooth.

6   Once cookies have cooled, spread white icing over one half of cookies, then spread chocolate icing over second half of cookies. You should use about 2 teaspoons of each icing per cookie. Let stand at room temperature until icing sets, about 1 hour, before serving.

DIY Ingredients

Dutch process cocoa will give the icing a very deep black color, but if you do not have it, you can use regular cocoa powder and a drop or two of black gel food coloring. Clear vanilla extract helps keep the white icing bright, but you can substitute pure vanilla extract.

TOASTER PASTRIES
The Sims 2

Running late getting your kids ready for the school bus in the morning? About to miss the 8 a.m. carpool? Throw some of these delicious Toaster Pastries in the oven and have a delicious breakfast ready in minutes. Just be careful not to burn down your kitchen!

Serves:	Prep Time:	Cook Time:
6	55 minutes	20 minutes

2 pre-made frozen piecrusts, thawed

1 cup fruit jam

2 teaspoons cornstarch

1 large beaten egg, divided

1 cup confectioners' sugar

1 tablespoon unsalted butter, melted

2 tablespoons whole milk

¼ teaspoon pure vanilla extract

2 tablespoons colored sprinkles

1 Preheat oven to 400°F and line a baking sheet with parchment paper.

2 On a work surface lightly dusted with flour, gently roll out each piecrust and cut each crust into six 4" x 3" rectangles.

3 In a small bowl, combine jam and cornstarch. Spread jam filling evenly on top of six piecrust rectangles. Brush edges of each fruit-topped rectangle with about ¼ teaspoon egg, then top with another piecrust rectangle. Press edges gently to seal.

4 Transfer rectangles to prepared baking sheet, cover with plastic wrap, and chill 15 minutes.

5 Once chilled, brush tops of each pastry with remaining egg. Bake 20 minutes or until pastries are puffed and golden brown on top and bottom. Cool on pan until just warm, about 20 minutes.

Continued on next page

6   While pastries bake, prepare icing. In a medium bowl, combine sugar, butter, milk, and vanilla. If icing seems too thick, add more milk ½ teaspoon at a time until desired consistency is reached.

7   Spoon icing over tops of cooled pastries and garnish with sprinkles. Serve warm or at room temperature.

CHOCOLATE CHIP COOKIES
The Sims 4

Picture this: You're looking to make a new friend in Oasis Springs, but you don't know how to find one. You decide to bring a delicious plate of Chocolate Chip Cookies to Johnny Zest's house. Instant best friends. It's a win-win: You both get cookies and a new friend. This recipe is absolutely perfect for that or any time a sweet craving hits.

Yields:	Prep Time:	Cook Time:
24 cookies	1 hour	10 minutes

½ cup unsalted butter, at room temperature

½ cup packed light brown sugar

2 tablespoons granulated sugar

1 large egg

½ teaspoon pure vanilla extract

1 cup all-purpose flour

½ teaspoon baking soda

¼ teaspoon salt

1 cup semisweet chocolate chips

1 Preheat oven to 350°F and line two baking sheets with parchment paper.

2 In a medium bowl with a hand mixer, add butter, brown sugar, and granulated sugar and mix on medium speed until creamy, about 1 minute. Add egg and vanilla and mix until well combined, about 30 seconds. Scrape down sides of bowl and set aside.

3 In a separate medium bowl, add flour, baking soda, and salt. Whisk to combine. Add flour to butter mixture and mix on low for 10 seconds, then increase speed to medium and mix until no dry ingredients remain, about 30 seconds. Scrape down sides of bowl as needed.

4 Add chocolate chips and fold in with a spatula. Use a heaping tablespoon to scoop batter onto prepared cookie sheets about 3" apart. Bake 8–10 minutes or until cookies are golden brown around edges and just set in center. Cool on pan 10 minutes before transferring to a wire rack to cool completely, about 30 minutes. Enjoy warm or at room temperature.

BERRY PIE

The Sims 2

You've probably had traditional pies like pumpkin, apple, or pecan, but have you ever tried Berry Pie? This pie takes whatever berries you love most and turns them into a delicious dessert that is incredible when served warm and with a scoop of vanilla ice cream on the side. You'll be coming back for seconds for sure.

Serves:	Prep Time:	Cook Time:
8	3 hours 45 minutes	58 minutes

1 (14.1-ounce) box prepared refrigerated piecrusts

½ cup plus 2 tablespoons granulated sugar, divided

¼ cup cornstarch

4 cups mixed fresh berries, such as strawberries, blueberries, and blackberries

2 teaspoons lemon juice

2 tablespoons whole milk

1 Remove one piecrust from package and unroll on a lightly floured work surface. Lay crust into a 9" pie plate and lift edges to help crust slide down sides of pan. Cover with plastic wrap and refrigerate while making berry mixture.

2 In a medium saucepan, add ½ cup sugar, cornstarch, and berries. Cook over medium heat until berry mixture comes to a boil and thickens, about 8 minutes. Stir in lemon juice, then remove from heat. Cool 15 minutes.

3 Preheat oven to 400°F and place a baking tray on rack in bottom third of oven.

4 Remove second piecrust and unroll on a lightly floured surface. Cut into eight 1" strips.

5 Remove first crust from refrigerator and uncover. Spoon berry filling into crust. Arrange piecrust strips over filling in a lattice pattern. Trim edge of crust to ½" and tuck under. Flute with fingers or crimp with a fork. Brush with milk and sprinkle over remaining 2 tablespoons sugar.

6   Place pie on baking tray in the oven. Bake 10 minutes, then reduce heat to 350°F and bake 35–40 minutes until filling is bubbling and crust is golden brown. Cool completely to room temperature, about 3 hours, before serving.

The Best Berries

The key to a great Berry Pie is in the berries, of course! If you plan to use fresh berries, you can use whatever mix of fruits is your favorite. However, if you're going to use frozen berries, be sure to stick with blueberries or strawberries for the best texture. You should also make sure to thaw the berries completely and get rid of excess liquid so as not to ruin the piecrust!

BEVERAGES

With every delicious meal, you need a delicious drink. The drinks in this chapter are going to knock your newly knitted socks off and will be a great pairing for the meal and treat recipes in previous chapters.

You don't even need to be a seasoned mixologist to create these drinks. All you need is a cup and the determination to improve your skill to create something beautiful. These recipes are inspired by so many parts of the game, including the gorgeous world of Sunset Valley and everyone's favorite character, the Freezer Bunny. Some drinks may leave you feeling warm and fuzzy, like Gnome's Sweet and Spicy, while others will leave you puckering up, like the Sour Punch. Whatever your drink preferences, there is something for you in this chapter. Grab yourself a bar shaped like a globe and get mixology-ing!

SUNSET VALLEY

The Sims 4

Named after an absolutely iconic town in *The Sims 3*, the Sunset Valley is a must-try beverage. This is the kind of drink Iliana Langerak would make each evening while Kaylynn sits and watches, thinking about her future plans to ruin the life of Daniel Pleasant and his wife before they'd ever even met—absolutely diabolical.

Serves:	Prep Time:	Cook Time:
1	5 minutes	N/A

1 ounce vanilla vodka

1 ounce heavy cream

½ ounce dark cocoa liqueur

½ ounce triple sec

Fill a highball glass with ice. Add all ingredients and stir well.

A Friendly Rivalry

In the description of Sunset Valley, you'll learn that the area was founded by the Goth family, but it was built up by the Landgraabs (of course). Now that the Altos have arrived, there is a pretty big rivalry between the Altos and the Landgraabs. These Sims had parallel lives, with their homes facing one another and both Nancy and Nick in the same career vying for that promotion. A true recipe for disaster!

DIM AND GUSTY
The Sims 4

The Dim and Gusty may not sound too appetizing, but you will not be disappointed. This drink appears with the **mixology** skill in *The Sims 4* and will impress any Sim who drinks it. The ginger beer gives it such a beautiful flavor, and the lime makes it taste so fresh and delicious!

Serves:	Prep Time:	Cook Time:
1	5 minutes	N/A

2 ounces bourbon

¼ ounce lime juice

2 ounces ginger beer

1 lime wedge

Fill a highball glass with ice. Add bourbon and lime juice and stir well. Add ginger beer and garnish with lime wedge.

SIMSMAPOLITAN
The Sims 4

This Sims-inspired Cosmopolitan is a delicious choice for your next outing and mixes so many citrusy and fruity flavors together perfectly.

Serves:	Prep Time:	Cook Time:
1	5 minutes	N/A

1 ounce citron vodka

1 ounce cranberry juice

½ ounce orange liqueur

¼ ounce lime juice

Fill a cocktail shaker with ice. Add all ingredients and shake 20 seconds. Strain into a martini glass.

Switch It Up!
If you aren't a fan of the taste of cranberry juice or just have another kind of juice in your fridge that you'd rather use, you can totally do that! Some of the best options are a cherry juice or fruit punch of your choice.

SALTY LAMA
The Sims 4

The Salty Llama appears as a mixology option in *The Sims 4* and is likely named after the llama mascot from *The Sims 3: University Life*. That llama would drop off a basket of goodies at your Sim's front door and probably felt salty after you didn't enroll. This coconutty drink could definitely make them happier!

Serves:	Prep Time:	Cook Time:
1	5 minutes	N/A

1½ **ounces coconut rum**

3 **ounces coconut water**

¼ **ounce lime juice**

Fill a tall glass with ice. Add all ingredients and stir well.

GNOME'S SWEET AND SPICY
The Sims 4

The Gnome's Sweet and Spicy may actually be the perfect drink for Sims who like a bit of spice but have yet to earn that coveted **spice hound** trait. Sip this on those hot summer days when you're worried about a fatal overheating and really need to cool down quickly to avoid a visit from the Grim Reaper.

Serves:	Prep Time:	Cook Time:
1	5 minutes	N/A

1½ ounces pepper vodka

2 ounces lemonade

Fill a highball glass with ice. Add ingredients and stir well.

GRANNY SMASH
The Sims 4

The apple doesn't fall far from the tree...it falls right into your glass! If you're a fan of apples, you'll definitely love the Granny Smash: It triples up on the apple flavor. With only a few ingredients you'll be able to whip this up in no time and start enjoying the rest of your night watching *Sims of the Dead* with your soulmate.

Serves:	Prep Time:	Cook Time:
1	5 minutes	N/A

1 ounce green apple vodka

½ ounce apple juice

¼ ounce green apple schnapps

Fill a cocktail shaker with ice. Add all ingredients and shake 20 seconds. Strain into a martini glass.

FREEZER BUNNY PUNCH
The Sims 4

Making their first appearance in the game inside of a community lot fridge, the Freezer Bunny has become a bit of a mascot for The Sims franchise. You'll find this little cutie hanging out in toy boxes, on your Sims phone screens, and even as tattoos in *The Sims 4*. Since this character is so iconic, they deserve their own drink!

Serves:	Prep Time:	Cook Time:
12	8 hours 10 minutes	N/A

1 (6-ounce) package strawberry gelatin

½ cup granulated sugar

2 cups boiling water

5 cups pineapple juice

5 cups cold water

1 (2-liter) bottle lemon-lime soda

1 In a large container with a tight-fitting lid, add gelatin, sugar, and boiling water. Mix until sugar and gelatin are dissolved.

2 Stir in pineapple juice and cold water and mix well. Cover with lid and place in freezer 8 hours or overnight.

3 To serve, stir in lemon-lime soda and pour into tall glasses. Enjoy immediately.

RIDGEPORT
The Sims 4

If you're looking for a deliciously fruity drink to enjoy at your next house party, look no further. The Ridgeport is a smooth beverage that features fruit punch and lime juice, making it perfect for sharing with friends! Just don't allow anyone to use their **mischief** skill to ruin the punch before your party guests get to enjoy it.

Serves:	Prep Time:	Cook Time:
1	5 minutes	N/A

1½ ounces gin or vodka

½ ounce lime juice

2 ounces fruit punch

1 lime wedge

Fill a highball glass with ice. Add gin or vodka, lime juice, and fruit punch and stir well. Garnish with lime.

LOVE POTION #4
The Sims 4

Are you headed to the Romance Festival because your last love interest abandoned you for a guy dressed in a llama costume? Well, you should definitely pack a bottle of Love Potion #4 in your bag for this important event. While it's not guaranteed to make any Sim fall in love with you, this drink is sure to impress. For an even more enticing presentation, serve this recipe in glass beakers!

Serves:	Prep Time:	Cook Time:
2	1 hour 5 minutes	N/A

2 tablespoons strawberry sorbet

6 ounces pink champagne

2 ounces pink lemonade

4 tablespoons whipped topping

1 teaspoon pink sugar sprinkles

1 Chill two champagne flutes in freezer 1 hour.

2 Remove flutes from freezer and add 1 tablespoon sorbet to each, then top with champagne, pink lemonade, whipped topping, and sprinkles. Serve immediately.

A Lovely Frozen Delight
Want to make this love potion even more delicious? You can swap out the whipped topping for a scoop of your favorite vanilla ice cream and turn it into a love potion float! This changes it up for a super-decadent experience that you'll be craving every day.

SOUR PUNCH
The Sims 4

If you're in the mood to pucker up, you should make a Sour Punch for your next beverage. Featuring simple syrup, lemon juice, and ginger ale, this sour drink is delicious. But you should probably avoid drinking it around Agnes Crumplebottom...she may think you're flirting, and that purse will go flying right at your head.

Serves:	Prep Time:	Cook Time:
1	5 minutes	N/A

½ ounce simple syrup

1 ounce fresh lemon juice

1½ ounces bourbon

1 ounce ginger ale

Fill a highball glass with ice. Add simple syrup and lemon juice and stir well. Add bourbon and stir to combine, then pour ginger ale over top.

The Language of The Sims

You may have noticed that the characters in the game aren't speaking a specific language, but their own language called Simlish. The reason for this is because the developers of the game thought it would get extremely repetitive if the characters were saying the same phrases over and over again in the language of the player.

SEA OF FIRE
The Sims 4

Featuring both hot pepper sauce and a pickled jalapeño, you may want to have a glass of milk handy when you enjoy the Sea of Fire. Just make sure you don't get that milk from a cow plant!

Serves:	Prep Time:	Cook Time:
1	5 minutes	N/A

1 ounce pepper vodka

4 ounces tomato juice

¼ teaspoon horseradish

3–4 dashes (⅛ teaspoon each) hot pepper sauce

4 dashes (½ teaspoon) Worcestershire sauce

1 dash (⅛ teaspoon) celery salt

1 pickled jalapeño

Fill a tall glass with ice. Add vodka, tomato juice, horseradish, hot pepper sauce, Worcestershire, and celery salt. Mix well. Place jalapeño on a toothpick and garnish glass.

A Friendly Scarecrow

In *The Sims 4: Seasons*, there is a cute object named Patchy the Straw Man who is a lot more than he seems. If your Sims interact with Patchy a whole bunch, they are eventually going to see Patchy leave their tree and come to life. Patchy will then start working on your garden if it needs it, and you can even be friends with or have romantic interactions with them.

US/METRIC CONVERSION CHART

VOLUME CONVERSIONS

US Volume Measure	Metric Equivalent
⅛ teaspoon	0.5 milliliter
¼ teaspoon	1 milliliter
½ teaspoon	2 milliliters
1 teaspoon	5 milliliters
½ tablespoon	7 milliliters
1 tablespoon (3 teaspoons)	15 milliliters
2 tablespoons (1 fluid ounce)	30 milliliters
¼ cup (4 tablespoons)	60 milliliters
⅓ cup	90 milliliters
½ cup (4 fluid ounces)	125 milliliters
⅔ cup	160 milliliters
¾ cup (6 fluid ounces)	180 milliliters
1 cup (16 tablespoons)	250 milliliters
1 pint (2 cups)	500 milliliters
1 quart (4 cups)	1 liter (about)

OVEN TEMPERATURE CONVERSIONS

Degrees Fahrenheit	Degrees Celsius
200 degrees F	95 degrees C
250 degrees F	120 degrees C
275 degrees F	135 degrees C
300 degrees F	150 degrees C
325 degrees F	160 degrees C
350 degrees F	180 degrees C
375 degrees F	190 degrees C
400 degrees F	205 degrees C
425 degrees F	220 degrees C
450 degrees F	230 degrees C

BAKING PAN SIZES

American	Metric
8 × 1½ inch round baking pan	20 × 4 cm cake tin
9 × 1½ inch round baking pan	23 × 3.5 cm cake tin
11 × 7 × 1½ inch baking pan	28 × 18 × 4 cm baking tin
13 × 9 × 2 inch baking pan	30 × 20 × 5 cm baking tin
2 quart rectangular baking dish	30 × 20 × 3 cm baking tin
15 × 10 × 2 inch baking pan	30 × 25 × 2 cm baking tin (Swiss roll tin)
9 inch pie plate	22 × 4 or 23 × 4 cm pie plate
7 or 8 inch springform pan	18 or 20 cm springform or loose bottom cake tin
9 × 5 × 3 inch loaf pan	23 × 13 × 7 cm or 2 lb narrow loaf or pâté tin
1½ quart casserole	1.5 liter casserole
2 quart casserole	2 liter casserole

INDEX

ABOUT THE AUTHOR

Taylor O'Halloran of Toronto, Canada, started playing The Sims with the first game back in 2000—and hasn't stopped since. Her love for the franchise inspired her to create *Ultimate Sims Guides*, a website full of tips and tricks for the game. It is now one of the biggest Sims resources available online. From there, she created a *YouTube* channel with over 50,000 subscribers—where she inspires players to play the game in new and exciting ways—as well as a *Twitch* stream, where viewers get to join in on the fun.